SOC
(Non)

FED UP!

Also by Rick Perry

On My Honor

FED UP!

Our Fight to Save America from Washington

RICK PERRY

Little, Brown and Company

NEW YORK   BOSTON   LONDON

Little, Brown and Company
Hachette Book Group
237 Park Avenue, New York, NY 10017
www.hachettebookgroup.com

First Edition: November 2010

Little, Brown and Company is a division of Hachette Book Group, Inc. The Little, Brown name and logo are trademarks of Hachette Book Group, Inc.

The publisher is not responsible for websites (or their contents) that are not owned by the publisher.

Library of Congress Cataloging-in-Publication Data
Perry, Rick.
    Fed up! : our fight to save America from Washington / Rick Perry.— 1st ed.
        p. cm.
    Includes bibliographical references and index.
    ISBN 978-0-316-13295-4 (hc)/ISBN 978-0-316-13346-3 (large print)
    1. Federal government—United States.   2. Central-local government relations—United States.   3. Decentralization in government—United States.   4. Liberty—United States.   I. Title.
JK325.P47 2010
320.520973—dc22   2010039666

10 9 8 7 6 5 4 3 2 1

RRD-IN

Printed in the United States of America

This book is dedicated to the great founders of this country and each generation of American patriots since who have understood that freedom is worth fighting for, and even dying for. To all the warriors who have poured out their blood on the altar of freedom, who have run to the sound of the guns because of devotion to country, I salute you. America is free because you were courageous.

This book is dedicated to the great founders of this country and each generation of American patriots since who have understood that freedom is worth fighting for, and even dying for. To all the warriors who have poured out their blood on the altar of freedom, who have run to the sound of the guns because of devotion to country, I salute you. America is free because you were courageous.

CONTENTS

CONTENTS

FOREWORD

I wish this book had never needed to be written.

It almost came too late.

America is recklessly accelerating toward economic disaster. *Fed Up!* may be the last warning sign to the danger that lies ahead.

Rick Perry, Texas governor for the past decade, is uniquely qualified to offer a firsthand perspective on why the United States — the most successful civilization in human history — is being threatened with economic collapse.

First Principles

Faith, freedom, and free enterprise are the pillars of a strong, safe, prosperous society. Rick knows that when these principles are protected, America succeeds, and when they are undermined, America fails. But the Left has a different belief. The Left believes that most people are not capable of pursuing happiness and that a strong centralized government is best able to provide for them. While claiming compassion for humanity, the Left's policies are destructive to the human beings subject to them — as we have had to learn painfully again and again.

The Left's self-serving solution to every crisis, economic or otherwise, and many of their own doing, is always the same: inflict higher taxes on Americans to create more government programs with more rules and regulations that result in less freedom, less innovation, less safety, and less prosperity.

The problem with the Left's one solution, as Rick forcefully explains in the pages that follow, is that it doesn't work. It's never worked, and it never will work. The record shows it.

But what the record also shows is that when power and freedom are returned to the people, when people are rewarded for work, and when government holds the line on spending, individuals and opportunity thrive. We have seen that result most spectacularly recently in Texas, and in the mid-1990s with the Contract with America Congress, when I served as Speaker of the House.

The Texas Record

Upon taking office, President Barack Obama repeatedly said that he was open to ideas on health care policy and on reversing the economic crisis. But he had to look no further than Texas to see ideas and policies that work.

Texas has no state income tax, no capital gains tax, and no tax on corporate dividends. In contrast, California taxes all three. It has the highest state income tax rates in the nation, with a top rate of 10.3 percent and with most income earners paying 9.3 percent. The California sales tax stands at 8.25 percent. In Texas, the state sales tax rate is 6.25 percent. With both the highest personal income tax and the highest state sales tax in the nation, California also has the largest budget deficit of any state.

Texas has economically outperformed California by any measure. Since 1998, economic growth in Texas has been nearly 20 percent higher than it is in California. Since the end of the tech boom, the rate of real economic growth in Texas has been 48.5 percent higher than in California. From 1998 to 2007, personal income in Texas grew 21 percent faster than in California. Since 2002, real personal income has grown 46 percent faster in Texas. From 2000 to 2007, California lost a net of 1.2 million residents. Texas, over the same period, gained more than half a million in interstate migration, the third highest in the country.

Prior to 2003, Texas was losing doctors at an alarming rate due to predatory practices of trial lawyers who were driving up the cost of malpractice insurance. In 2003, the Texas legislature passed a measure to limit medical liability. In that same year, a state constitutional amendment was approved by voters to cap noneconomic damages awarded by juries. These two provisions reversed the trend and improved care, accessibility, and the overall economy by making Texas a more attractive place to live, work, and own a business. Malpractice claims dropped, and physician recruitment and retention went up. Doctors saved more than $50 million on insurance premiums, and hospitals' insurance rates went down.

People in Texas, like anyone living in any state, have a choice. They can vote with their feet. Many living in California simply became fed up with their state's high taxes and regulations. Many who moved out moved to Texas, where on average they are safer, freer, and more prosperous. Competition among the states is a powerful incentive for states to keep taxes and the cost of doing business low. And as this California versus Texas example shows, conservative economic policies work and socialist policies don't.

Yet both the Obama administration and the Pelosi-Reid

Congress continue to ignore success stories like Texas. They are going in the opposite direction, passing a massive government takeover of health care while planning similarly massive tax increases to pay for it and for the rest of their job-killing agenda.

Now, it may not be surprising that a politician from Chicago would not naturally look to the Lone Star State for solutions. And you wouldn't expect a Texas governor to look in Illinois for answers (thankfully).

And that is precisely the point of this book. States have been called laboratories in democracy precisely because every problem potentially has fifty different approaches to solving it. Some solutions work in some states and not in others. Some states prefer some solutions over others. Some solutions may work in every state, and some just don't work at all. But the best way to find the best solutions is to allow the states to discover what works best for them, without the federal government interfering.

In today's global economy, each state is competing not only with other states for businesses, workers, and investors but also on a global level. The fact is, with the right principles and policies, you can make any place rich, as happened in Hong Kong.

Unfortunately, the opposite applies as well. With the wrong principles and the wrong policies, you can make any place poor, as happened in Detroit. In 1950, 1.8 million people called Detroit home. It ranked first in median income of all major cities in America. But after Detroit's political leaders, ignoring the principles of freedom and free markets, governed with runaway government spending and taxes, Detroit shrank by more than half. Today, the Motor City is number 66 in median household income in a list of 68 major American cities. One-third of its residents are living below the poverty line, and the unemployment rate is the highest of any major metropolitan area in the country.

The Record of the Contract with America Congress

The Left's willful ignorance of the historical record concerning principles and policies that work is not limited to Texas. The Left also ignores the success of the Contract with America Congress from just fifteen years ago.

Beginning in 1995, after the Republicans gained the majority in both Houses of Congress, the policies generated by the Contract with America set out to put America back on the road to prosperity and keep it there.

Among the historic accomplishments of this Congress were congressional accountability, welfare reform, fewer regulations, the lowest increase in federal spending since the 1920s, the first tax cuts in sixteen years, and the first four consecutive balanced budgets (reducing the public debt by over $400 billion) since the 1920s.

The federal deficit went from $107.4 billion in 1996 to a $125.6 billion surplus in 1999. During that time, unemployment dropped 1.4 percent, from 5.6 to 4.2 percent, with the creation of 8.4 million new jobs. The Dow Jones Industrial Average (DJIA) rose 140 percent, from 3,834 to 9,213, between January 1995 and January 1999.

By comparison, since 2008, the Democrat-controlled Congress has added an astonishing $4.6 trillion to the public debt, including $1.6 trillion in 2010 alone. Nearly 7 million jobs have been destroyed under the Pelosi-Reid Congresses between January 2007 and June 2010. Unemployment has risen 4.9 percent, from 4.6 to 9.5 percent. And would be 10.4 percent if it included discouraged workers, those individuals who are unemployed but are not actively seeking employment, usually because they have had no success finding a job after searching for a long time. The total number of unemployed and underemployed workers in July 2010 stood at an astonishing 26 million. Between January 2007 and August 2010, the DJIA dropped 1,823 points.*

During the 1990s, at the same time that the Republicans were cutting taxes, we were also cutting spending. As a share of the gross domestic product (GDP), federal spending fell from 20.2 percent in fiscal year 1996 to 18.5 percent in FY 1999. But even as the economy grew dramatically from 1994 to 1999, federal revenue as a percentage of GDP actually increased. That is, even with lower taxes and a higher GDP, more money came into the federal treasury.

The Pelosi-Reid Congresses have increased spending as a share of the GDP from 20.7 percent in FY 2008 to 25.4 percent in FY 2010, the highest since it spiked in FY 1945, at the end of World War II. Between FY 2007 (the last Republican budget) and FY 2011 Congress has increased spending by a total of $1.105 trillion.†

Since World War II, the average duration of a recession had been ten months, with the longest lasting sixteen months. July 2010 marked thirty-one months since the current recession began, and we're still losing jobs.‡ Yet despite this fact, the Pelosi-Reid Congress has set in motion comprehensive, across-the-board tax-rate increases for next year on both businesses and investors that will extend the downturn indefinitely.

---

* *Sources:* Office of Management and Budget, Bureau of Labor Statistics, and Dow Jones.
† *Source:* Office of Management and Budget.
‡ *Source:* National Bureau of Economic Research.

Moving Power Back to the People

The evidence of what works and what doesn't is empirically irrefutable, yet the ideologically stubborn Keynesians in the Obama administration and the Pelosi-Reid Congress refuse to acknowledge it. They ignore both the Texas success under Governor Perry's leadership and the Contract with America success in the 1990s.

Instead of pursuing the policies that have time and again demonstrated success, the Obama administration and the Pelosi-Reid Congress insist on following job-killing economic policies rather than the job-creating policies that we know work. Chief among these job-killing policies are a failed trillion-dollar stimulus package and the bound-to-fail "Obamacare."

Unfortunately for America, the Obama administration is creating a job-killing economic system based on an ideology of centralizing power, which most people considered a failure after the collapse of the Soviet Union. These failed policies have brought us to the edge of the cliff. This gets us back to the importance of moving power away from Washington and back to the states and the local level.

For most of our history, Washington was a far-off place that had little influence on the daily lives of most Americans. More recently, the federal government has usurped or seduced enormous power away from local and state governments. There are in the United States today 513,000 elected local, state, and federal officials, but only 537 are elected on the federal level, or about one-tenth of 1 percent. Yet so much power has been consolidated in the hands of federally elected officials, as well as in the hands of unelected bureaucrats and federal judges. We need to reverse this trend or we will suffer lasting consequences.

FOREWORD

Devolving power out of Washington is critical to our long-term survival. Rick has done a great service by explaining how we got here and what we can do about it. His position as governor of Texas gives him a tremendous platform for helping us change course and return to sound conservative fiscal policies. But he can't do it alone. Every American has a duty to rein in the out-of-control federal government. *Fed Up!* is your handbook. It will arm you with the facts so that you can inform your family, friends, and neighbors. An informed citizenry is the best tool we have in the arsenal to defend our Republic.

Newt Gingrich, August 2010

PREFACE

I grew up in Paint Creek, Texas. If you can't find it on a map, I won't be surprised. Just look for Haskell, Texas, population 3,000, and then go a few miles to the south and the east and you *might* find it. We were cotton farmers. We believed in God, we believed in taking care of ourselves and one another, and we believed that America was the greatest nation on earth. We still do.

Serving as the governor of Texas for almost ten years has given me a unique perspective on the current state of things in our country. And from my vantage point, I see a nation filled with good, hardworking people who are wondering what happened to the country they knew. It wasn't so long ago that we were expected to pay our bills, we were able to pray at the town meeting, and we believed it was important to rely on ourselves or our families rather than government.

Now, cynics will say that I decided to write this book because I seek higher office. They are wrong: I already have the best job in America. I wrote this book because I believe that America is great but also that America is in trouble — and heading for a cliff if we don't take immediate steps to change course. I wrote this book in the hopes that it will lead to a new conversation about the proper role of government in our lives and perhaps be a step toward renewing our collective appreciation for the genius of our nation's federal system of government—when it works the way it is supposed to.

I believe that government is best when it is closest to the people. I believe that states are the critical components of our federal system of government, that the Founders recognized their importance, and that empowering the states is the best way to ensure our God-given right to live according to the dictates of our consciences. I believe that we have let establishment politicians on both sides of the aisle empower Washington at the expense of states, and thus our liberty. I believe that our fight today is to restore the proper balance of power in order to ensure that America can remain free and prosperous—and capable of continuing to lead the world.

FED UP!

1

America Is Great, Washington Is Broken

*A Constitution of Government once changed
from Freedom, can never be restored. Liberty, once lost,
is lost forever.*

— JOHN ADAMS, LETTER TO ABIGAIL ADAMS,
JULY 17, 1775[1]

SOMETHING IS TERRIBLY WRONG. There is a sense
among Americans that the world we have always known is in
danger of being turned upside down.

Now, do not misunderstand me. America is great. Our nation
has done, and continues to do, more for the cause of freedom
around the world than any nation in the history of man. And our
nation is filled with people, whether they were born here or came
here in search of the American dream, who are driven by faith,
determination, personal responsibility, and self-reliance. They are
forging better lives for themselves and their children. This is the
land of opportunity—a place where, after all, a rural cotton
farmer from Paint Creek, Texas, can become governor.

Americans have fed more people, clothed more people, healed
more people, and improved the lives of more people—and more
quickly—than any other society the world has known. And we

have done it by believing in the individual, by defending liberty, no matter the price, and by demonstrating a living, abiding faith that has compelled us throughout the generations to act against evil and to advance good.

But America is in trouble, and the people know it. We sense that our way of life and, perhaps more importantly, our ability to decide how we shall live, is no longer in our control but in the control of an increasingly powerful and oppressive national government—a government run by people who simply do not share our values or our beliefs and blatantly ignore its limits.

In short, it is not America that is broken; it is Washington that is broken.

You can't argue with the fact that power has increasingly been consolidated in Washington. In 1960, the government of the United States spent approximately $92 billion annually, or $509 per person. By 1987, that figure had grown to $1 trillion, or $4,127 per person. This year, federal spending is projected to surpass $3.7 trillion, or $11,500 per person.[2] There are over 2 million civilian federal employees, an additional 1.5 million in the U.S. military (that part is a good thing), and millions more involved in federal contracts. There are over 4,500 independent federal criminal laws and over 163,000 pages of federal regulations scattered across hundreds of agencies in 15 different departments.[3] The federal tax code and its supporting regulations total over 9 million words across thousands of pages.[4]

The federal government is massive and grows more so by the day. Indeed, by the end of the 111th Congress, there will likely be more than 6,500 new bills introduced in the House of Representatives and 4,000 more in the Senate, designed, ostensibly, to cure the nation's ills.[5]

Of course, it never occurs to the power brokers in Washington that perhaps they are the cause of much of what ails us. But it does occur to the American people. I have had the privilege of meeting and talking with tens of thousands of my fellow citizens from all walks of life, and I can tell you one thing for certain: the American people are fed up.

We are fed up with being overtaxed and overregulated. We are tired of being told how much salt we can put on our food, what windows we can buy for our house, what kind of cars we can drive, what kinds of guns we can own, what kind of prayers we are allowed to say and where we can say them, what political speech we are allowed to use to elect candidates, what kind of energy we can use, what kind of food we can grow, what doctor we can see, and countless other restrictions on our right to live as we see fit.

We are fed up with a federal government that has the arrogance to preach to us about how to live our lives, and the chutzpah to haul every baseball player and other "evildoer" in the world before a congressional committee—or some comic such as Stephen Colbert. Meanwhile, Congress, arguably one of the most incompetent regimes with one of the worst track records of mismanagement in the history of mankind, runs up over $13 trillion and counting in debt.

We are fed up with bailout after bailout and stimulus plan after stimulus plan, each one of which tosses principle out the window along with taxpayer money. We can't even keep up with all the spending, be it the $700 billion Troubled Asset Relief Program (TARP), the auto industry bailout, the AIG bailout, or President Obama's failed $787 billion "Recovery Act." The list goes on and on.

We are fed up with a federal government that pledged $200 billion to bail out Fannie Mae and Freddie Mac when their mismanagement, coupled with ridiculous federal regulations, led to the inappropriate lending policies underlying the financial crisis in the first place. And we are fed up with tax credits that amount to pure giveaways to certain citizens at the expense of others—the government picking winners and losers based on circumstance and luck with no real benefit to the economy.

We are fed up with a Department of Homeland Security that refuses to secure our borders, resulting in more than 10 million people living in our country illegally, thousands more coming in daily from all over the world, and almost 1,000 children being born in our country every day to parents who are here illegally.[6] Meanwhile, politicians use the issue of immigration as a political tool to divide Americans.

We are fed up with a self-interested Congress that spends its time earmarking over 9,000 pet projects in 2010 worth over $16 billion, a number Democrats tout as an accomplishment because it represents just over half of the peak amount of $29 billion under Republicans in 2006—all of which corrupts the political process and wastes our money.[7]

We are fed up with a Congress that often fails to even read the legislation it passes and that increasingly writes laws, such as the health care bill, that are over 2,000 pages long.

We are fed up with activist judges who tell us what is right and wrong and deny us the right to live as we see fit—from deciding when life begins and where the Ten Commandments can be displayed to telling the people how to punish criminals.

We are fed up that Social Security and Medicare teeter on the verge of bankruptcy, amassing unfathomable liabilities for future generations, that the federal government refuses to admit it, and that there is no leadership in Washington to do anything about it—unless you count yet another committee chaired by a retired senator that will no doubt be appointed to fix them.

We are fed up with a federal government arrogant enough to declare it knows more about our health than our doctor and that is willing to risk the best health care system in the world while blatantly lying that it is not on the path to a single-payer, government-run system.

But perhaps most of all we are fed up because deep down we know how great America has always been, how many great things the people have done in spite of their government, and how great the nation can be in the future if government will just get out of the way.

America *is* great. Yet for some in our nation, to make such a statement is considered arrogant, close-minded, or jingoistic — the kind of thing said by cowboys, as if it is a bad thing to be a cowboy.

At a press conference in Strasbourg in April 2009, President Barack Obama said in response to a question about the traditional notion of American exceptionalism, "I believe in American exceptionalism, just as I suspect that the Brits believe in British exceptionalism and the Greeks believe in Greek exceptionalism."[8]

You got the first half right, Mr. President, but even if Greece were not facing an economic meltdown, I still believe that America is unique in its greatness. I believe that it *is* exceptional, and has been ever since its founding, because of its reliance on and belief in the individual, in liberty, in equal justice under law, in God, in a limited constitutional government, and in the willingness of its people to risk their lives in defense of those things around the world.

It is this willingness to defend liberty and answer the call of duty that most defines the exceptionalism of America. After I graduated from college at Texas A&M University in 1972, I was blessed to serve over four years in the United States Air Force flying C-130s. That experience had a profound impact on me and remains one of the proudest accomplishments of my life. But as proud as I am of that service, I confess that I stand in awe of the men and women in uniform today who are answering our country's call.

One of the greatest parts about being governor of Texas is the time I get to spend meeting with those brave men and women, be it in my visits to the many great bases throughout the state, or in my travels overseas to such places as Iraq and Afghanistan. When I spend time with those who are putting their lives on the line in defense of liberty and our nation, I know that the great World War II generation has some competition for the title "greatest." Never is that reality clearer than when I talk to the family of a young man or woman who has paid the ultimate sacrifice in defense of liberty.

These brave Americans are following in the footsteps of the generations that came before them. America has always answered the call to defend freedom. Throughout the past century, over 600,000 Americans have given their lives in defense of liberty, almost none of whom perished on American soil. More than another million were wounded during that time. And what have we asked for in return? Land. But not land taken in conquest—rather only, as General Colin Powell once noted, "enough land to bury our dead."[9] One need only take a trip to Normandy, France, where 9,387 Americans are buried—including thirty-three pairs of brothers buried side by side—under a sea of crosses and Stars of David, to realize our willingness to sacrifice.[10]

Just as no other nation in the history of mankind has sacrificed or given more for the cause of liberty or the pursuit of justice throughout the world, no other country has done more to promote economic prosperity or to improve the global standard of living than has ours. I have witnessed the greatness of America's economic engine and her generosity firsthand. Thousands of entrepreneurs and hardworking Americans are laboring as we speak to create jobs and build the economy. The United States of America accounts for about 6 percent of the world's landmass and less than 5 percent of its people, yet its economy generates almost 25 percent of global gross domestic product.[11]

Americans have won more Nobel Prizes than the citizens of any other country, a total of 38 percent of all Nobel Prizes awarded.[12] The United States ranks among the freest economies in the world, and according to rankings published annually since 1973 by Freedom House for political freedom, civil liberties, and freedom of the press, the United States has received the highest possible rating each year since the inception of the survey.

Thousands of Americans are working every day to make the best health care system in the world even better, and saving countless lives in the process. The United States is the home of medical innovations ranging from the polio vaccine to the artificial heart. Thanks to the efforts of the March of Dimes and Dr. Jonas Salk, in 1994 polio was declared eradicated in all of the Americas. The measles vaccine was also invented in the United States, and endemic transmission of measles (among other formerly deadly diseases) has been virtually eliminated in the United States. The United States is home to about half of the 20 largest pharmaceutical companies in the world.[13] More than 90 scientists either born or working in the United States have won the Nobel Prize in Physiology or Medicine.[14]

And because America is historically a country dedicated to freedom and equal justice under law, and also a country of opportunity, innovation, and invention, where our people are free to prosper as they push the boundaries of science and commerce, the lines at our door are long, and growing longer. Well over 3 million people from around the world are on a waiting list for a chance to come here to pursue the American dream, and some of those people have been on that list for 20 years.[15] Still millions more risk imprisonment—or even their lives—to come here illegally, which, besides being a problem in and of itself, is indicative of how badly people want to come to this great nation.

I am particularly proud of the job states like Texas have done and continue to do in the face of the economic challenges that have gripped our nation in recent years. We know that the route to success is lower taxes, smaller government, and freedom for every individual, because we have seen it work. Indeed, the well-known economist Ray Perryman has pegged Texas as the "last in and first out" of this current economic crisis because of our job growth at the end of 2009 and an unemployment rate that has stayed well below the national average.

Indeed, the Texas unemployment rate is the lowest among the nation's ten largest states, as is our state's level of debt, according to *Forbes* magazine. We have also produced more private-sector jobs than any other state in the nation over the past ten years, and earlier this year, Texas was named the top exporting state in the country for the eighth straight year. That's what happens when you free up citizens to compete. And as a result, we were able to finish our last legislative session with a balanced budget, a tax cut for 40,000 small businesses, and over $8 billion set aside for our state's "rainy-day fund." In fact, Texas and Alaska are responsible for two-thirds of all state dollars set aside in reserve. A sad indictment on the rest of America, this is a source of pride for those of us in Austin.

This is not to say Texas and Texans aren't struggling, too. But by remaining committed to the idea that Americans prosper when left free from government interference, and by remaining patient and working hard, Texas is leading the nation through the economic turmoil.

Beyond our economy, our greatness in Texas and throughout America is observed in the character of our people. Take a moment to consider the outpouring of love and charity demonstrated by the citizens of my state and others around the nation to those desperate souls suffering in the wake of Hurricane Katrina and countless other devastating events. The people of Harris County did not hesitate to welcome as many as 200,000 residents of New Orleans, processing tens of thousands of evacuees and working hard to find shelter, food, clothes, medicine, and other basic necessities.

Americans freely give billions of dollars, volunteer countless hours, and otherwise devote their lives to help those here at home and around the world who are in need. Of course, the U.S. government consistently contributes more toward overseas aid than the government of any other country, but what is far more impressive is the amount individual Americans give in voluntary donations. U.S. private giving to poor nations reached $37.3 billion in 2008.[16] The next highest were the United Kingdom and Germany, which each gave less than $2 billion. Total charitable giving in the United States is estimated by the Giving USA Foundation to be $303.74 billion in 2009, exceeding $300 billion for the third consecutive year.[17]

There has never been a challenge our nation has not risen to meet, driven by a people blessed by the Almighty and given by our forefathers a historically limited government that frees the individual to achieve greatness. That is the story of our America.

So America is great, and it's worth saving. But what are we saving it from? In the largest sense, we're saving it from Washington. Our "historically limited government" no longer is very limited; in fact, it has been turned on its head.

The Constitution established a general government of limited, enumerated powers specifically to prevent the consolidation of power in Washington and to leave all remaining powers with the states or the people. This important concept was purposefully memorialized in the Bill of Rights. The Tenth Amendment to the Constitution reads:

The powers not delegated to the United States by the Constitution, nor prohibited by it to the States, are reserved to the States respectively, or to the people.

But the endless arrogance in Washington demonstrates a total disrespect for the Constitution and for the limits on federal power that the Constitution requires. By forsaking the very framework of government given to us by the Founders, we have allowed government to control us instead of controlling the government ourselves. The American people are increasingly aware of this and find it maddening.

It is not just the separation of powers among the executive, legislative, and judicial branches that limits the consolidation of power. What was particularly ingenious of the Founders was their crafting of a unique form of government that also spread power between the state and the general governments—both sovereigns, if you will. Dividing the government's authority preserves liberty, and by limiting the general government's powers and leaving the rest to the states, the Founders made sure that most decision making would be handled at the level closest to, and most accountable to, the people.

Ask yourself this: are you most likely to gain the attention of the President or your local mayor? Your U.S. senator or your local city councilman? Your congressman or your local state representative? The answer is obvious. Your city council, your mayor, your local school board, and often even your state representative are people who live and work in your neighborhood. These are people you are likely to be able to influence and whom you can more easily hold accountable. So, is it better for them or for Washington to have more power over your life? The Founders knew the answer to this question over two hundred years ago, and they were right.

We can all still be proud Americans while acknowledging that we simply do not agree on many fundamental issues. We are a diverse people—incapable of being governed from a faraway capital by people who do not share our values. Recognizing this fact is critical to the preservation of a free state. Federalism enables us to live united as a nation, with a federal government that is focused on our national security and that has specific enumerated powers, while we live in states with like-minded people who share our values and beliefs. Crucial to understanding federalism in modern-day America is the concept of mobility, or "the ability to vote with your feet." If you don't support the death penalty and citizens packing a pistol, don't come to Texas. If you don't like medicinal marijuana and gay marriage, don't move to California.

For too long, the silent majority has sat idly by, allowing the political establishment to wage an assault not just on the Constitution and the fundamental American principle of limited government, but on the very idea that it is a government closest to the people that best guarantees the blessings of liberty.

The political establishment responsible for this assault consists primarily of two camps.

First, there are those who believe in the primacy of the government over the individual, referred to as liberals, so-called Progressives, or statists. I do not care which descriptor you use—whether they are Democrat or Republican, whether they are well intentioned or ill-, whether they deny it or not—they simply do not believe in those things that have made our nation the greatest in the history of the world. They do not believe what I believe.

The statists believe in a powerful, activist central government that advances a radical secular agenda in the name of compassion. They hide behind misguided notions of empathy and push token talking points about fighting for "the little guy," all the while empowering the federal government to coercively and blatantly undermine state-, local-, and self-governance.

Second, there are those who enable the statists—a group largely made up of old-guard Republicans, sometimes professing a questionable belief in conservatism—who are complicit in expanding Washington at the expense of the states and the people. They cowardly and selfishly empower themselves politically by compromising liberty issue by issue, often selling principle for a bridge, a museum, or some building named after them back in their home district or state. It is not enough to pay lip service to limited government or conservative principles if you go forward promoting and embracing flawed, misguided policies that expand the size and scope of the federal government.

Now, let me clear up one thing. I am a proud Republican. As frustrated as I am at many in my own party for their waste and incompetence, and as many good friends as I have in the Democratic Party, I am firmly convinced that there is no comparison between the two political parties in modern, twenty-first-century America. As I have said before, "Republicans often aren't on the right page—indeed, some aren't even in the right chapter. But most are in the right book. Most Democrats today, on the other hand, can't even find the library."

And what I mean by that is simple. Republicans, in general, believe in low taxes, low regulation, less spending, free-market health care, constitutionalist judges, protecting innocent life, enforcing our laws and our borders, peace through strength, empowering the states, and generally advocating principles closer to limited government than not. On the other hand, most of my Democrat friends—unfortunately—generally believe in higher taxes, more regulation, more spending, government-run health care, activist judges, choice over life, open borders, capitulation to our enemies, a more powerful Washington, and generally a bigger and more active government than not.

The truth is, I really don't care what party the statist is in. The fact of the matter is, it is the statist, and those who support or enable him, who is the problem. For too long he has undermined this country by empowering the national government at the expense of liberty. An America defined by the statist in Washington is an America doomed to fail.

But I don't believe that is our fate. I believe in an America defined by the people and by the concept of liberty, an America that will prosper and continue to lead the world. I believe in an America that will stand up to and call out the establishment for what they are, and will change the course of history by stripping them of their power at the ballot box and by exercising the power of the states to stop blindly accepting every demand the federal government makes.

It is the call of our generation—of you and me—to fight to preserve, as Ronald Reagan referred to our great nation, "the last best hope of man on earth." At stake is the birthright of our children—their right to proudly proclaim that they are American and for that to be synonymous with liberty and the willingness to sacrifice for it. At stake is the future not just of our nation but, the future of self-government and the right of the people to live free according to the dictates of their conscience.

In short, it is not enough to be fed up. We must act.

Hundreds of thousands of patriotic Americans have taken to the streets in protest—invoking the historic Boston Tea Party in the process. They are running for office and swarming the voting booths, sending shock waves from Massachusetts to Hawaii. Their anger is directed against the establishment—that lumbering mass of old-guard politicians who do not understand that there is a quiet revolution taking place. And the shock waves are being felt on both sides of the political aisle.

These are the political winds that shape our time. We have now seen in several consecutive elections that the American people are indeed fed up. Over the course of just two elections, Republicans lost 14 seats in the U.S. Senate and 53 seats in the U.S. House between 2006 and 2008. This year, however, the situation has reversed, and Republicans are the ones who have gained seats.

This is just the beginning of our fight. Our cause is simple: to restore the balance of power intended by our Founders but forsaken by secular progressives determined to say what government will do for the people rather than allowing people to do what they can do for themselves. Our goal is to take power away from Washington and instead empower states, communities, and individuals, because America's future greatness is inextricably intertwined with states pushing back.

Our Founding Fathers had a vision of states working together but also competing against one another to put different ideas in play, seeing which ones work, which ones don't, and then allowing governors and legislatures to look around and say, "You know what? That's a good idea over there." Restoring that vision will enable us to live according to our beliefs and our values—and to prosper according to the fruits of our labor, free from interference from a faraway bureaucrat, legislator, or judge.

Our fight to save America from Washington might well be the last chance for the last best hope of man on earth. America the people, and America the idea, endure. Whether they continue to endure is up to us. The good news is that the American people always rise to a challenge.

2

Why States Matter

*Were not this great country already divided into states,
that division must be made, that each might do for itself
what concerns itself directly, and what it can so much
better do than a distant authority.*

— THOMAS JEFFERSON, *Autobiography*[1]

WHY DO STATES MATTER? In fact, why even have states at
all? Why establish a boundary between Virginia and Maryland
or between Texas and Oklahoma? Why bother with separate
governments—choosing to drive with a South Carolina driver's
license, attend a Texas school, obtain a license to practice law or
medicine in New York, get a hunting license in Alaska, or get
married with a license in Georgia? Why empower states instead
of having a single, powerful national government?

The simplest answer is this: Americans want to live free. They
want to gather together with people of common beliefs and goals
to establish communities in which they can prosper. They do not
want to be told how to live their lives. They certainly don't want
some faraway bureaucrat, judge, or representative of a different
community to tell them how to live. That liberty has been the
essence of America ever since the colonists came here.

Our ancestors set forth to forge a nation from the wilderness of a newly discovered land and endured massive hardships to do it. They cultivated the land and built roads and bridges, churches and schools, businesses and homes, to form the communities in which Americans live today. And while colonies certainly developed under the Crown, they also developed independently, with their own governors, legislatures, and constitutions, and became the vehicles by which communities were established. Each was independent and mostly autonomous. After the original Articles of Confederation failed to provide adequate power for national defense and trade, the colonies-turned-states acceded to the ratification of the Constitution with the guarantee that the powers of the central government be limited and that the states retain their sovereignty.

In fact, our name says it all. While some countries may have a similar structure of government on paper, such as Austria, or may have states referenced in their official name, such as the United Mexican States, they are otherwise only really known as Austria or Mexico. The United States of America is the only nation consistently referred to by its very structure. Indeed, when someone abroad says "the United States," or even simply "the States," most people know what is meant. This is so because our unique empowerment of states and recognition of their role in protecting liberty set the country apart from the beginning.

Empowering States to Promote Liberty

The Founders recognized that forming a strong union requires the preservation of liberty, and that the preservation of liberty requires a government located closest to the people. This is the essence of our great nation. That the Founders sought to empower states broadly while limiting the federal government is beyond dispute. James Madison, generally regarded as the Father of the Constitution, when arguing for ratification of the Constitution in *Federalist 45,* said:

The powers delegated by the proposed Constitution to the federal government are few and defined. Those which are to remain in the state governments are numerous and indefinite. The former will be exercised principally on external objects, as war, peace, negotiation, and foreign commerce; and which last the power of taxation will for the most part be connected. The powers reserved to the several states will extend to all the objects which, in the ordinary course of affairs, concern the lives, liberties, and properties of the people, and the internal order, improvement, and prosperity of the State.

The operations of the Federal Government will be most extensive and important in times of war and danger; those of the state governments, in times of peace and security.[2]

This power structure is no trivial matter. It is not a footnote to our founding or something just for the history books. It is the result of intense forethought and debate by the very men who pledged their lives, their fortunes, and their sacred honor to give this nation to us. This structure protects the liberty of every American while honoring the cohesive whole we are as a nation.

An obvious question arises, though: how do the states protect liberty, and what is liberty in the first place? Well, before there was government, there were people. We, the people, were given life by our Creator. With life came curiosity, the capacity to reason, and the ability to translate our dreams into reality. Each of us is unique and possesses the free will to make our own choices and moral decisions. But that common gift of life unites us and requires of us the mutual respect necessary to form the societies in which we live. With the founding of the United States came the express notion that those societies should be built upon the central pillar of freedom.

This is the essence of liberty in America. Through freedom and mutual respect, each of us is free to pursue our dreams and to become the best versions of ourselves, together creating a community of people reaching their highest God-given potential. And the idea that government exists to serve the will of the people — to further individual freedom rather than the appetites of rulers — is what made the American system unique and attractive to people around the globe.

Now, some claim that there can be too much liberty or that people cannot be trusted if they have too much freedom. I do not believe that is true. The kind of liberty we construe as harmful is not really liberty but rather license. And license serves only the selfish appetite at the expense of others. Liberty is a God-given virtue; license is a destructive vice fomented by the forces of evil. If liberty were to include the freedom to harm others, then of course that would be too much of it. But within liberty's essence is a recognition of the inherent value of other human beings. This "rightful" liberty is the blessing that our federal system of government was established to preserve and protect. Liberty is our birthright as Americans. It exists within moral boundaries that protect the rights of others. As Jefferson said:

> Of liberty I would say that, in the whole plenitude of its extent, it is unobstructed action according to our will. But rightful liberty is unobstructed action according to our will within limits drawn around us by the equal rights of others. I do not add "within the limits of the law," because law is often but the tyrant's will, and always so when it violates the right of an individual.[3]

Liberty's Origins in America and Its Founding Documents

Liberty guides present-day America because it was the colonists' founding principle. By the mid-1700s, thirteen separate colonies had coalesced out of the varying religious and economic interests of their settlers and had largely become self-governing entities with unique identities. While England was the ultimate authority, much was left to local determination, which helped establish a culture of independence.

In common among the colonies, however, was the extent to which they became increasingly fed up with an oppressive British government located 3,000 miles away dictating how they should live. Taxes and impositions placed on the colonists without their consent were just some of the "long train of abuses" that led in 1775 to the firing of shots at Lexington and the subsequent formation of the Second Continental Congress. With reverberating eloquence the following year, the delegates made known through the Declaration of Independence that "Governments are instituted among Men, deriving their just powers from the consent of the governed." The colonists would not be subjects of a tyrannical king—or Parliament—that controlled their lives, liberty, and pursuits of happiness without having either solicited their input or won their approval. And for that liberty, they would fight.

Recognizing that casting off an imperial power such as Britain would require greater coordination, the Second Continental Congress immediately set out to draft a new constitution while continuing to manage the war effort. By 1777, the Articles of Confederation had passed the Congress but were not ratified by all thirteen states until 1781. The primary purpose of this union was to form a compact of allegiance among the colonies to provide for their common defense and security. Notably absent from the Articles was the authority for the national government to tax or enforce economic regulation. No executive or judicial function was established for this national government, so jealous of their newly asserted liberties were the Founding Fathers. In fact, the Founders included the following fail-safe provision in the Articles: "Each state retains its sovereignty, freedom, and independence, and every power, jurisdiction, and right, which is not by this Confederation expressly delegated to the United States, in Congress assembled."[4]

After the war against England was won, however, a number of our nation's early leaders began to point out deficiencies in the Articles of Confederation. First, the national government had amassed significant war debt during the Revolution, but it was not empowered by the Articles to compel the payment of taxes by either the states or the people. Rather, it was able to only request money from the states, which, also deep in debt, were loath to pay. Second, because the national government was not empowered to regulate commerce among the states, states passed protectionist legislation, including debtor-relief laws that imposed significant burdens on other states and impeded the free flow of goods and economic growth throughout the country. The problems got out of hand, leading to insurrections like Shays' Rebellion in Massachusetts and prompting reconsideration of the balance of power and the desired level of peacetime coordination among the states.

The result was the Philadelphia Convention of 1787, to which state delegates were sent to amend the Articles of Confederation. What resulted, of course, was a redrafting rather than amendment of the document, and the creation of the Constitution of the United States. While the new national government was significantly more empowered under the Constitution than its predecessor had been, the Founders sought to explicitly codify a system of government that preserved the integrity of the states and guaranteed individual rights through a federal system. As James Madison explained in *Federalist 39,* "Each State, in ratifying the Constitution, is considered as a sovereign body, independent of all others, and only to be bound by its own voluntary act. In this relation, then, the new Constitution will, if established, be a *federal,* and not a national constitution."[5]

So, do states matter? The Founders clearly thought so. The Constitution guaranteed a federal government of enumerated powers while leaving states with governments of residual and plenary power. States have the prerogative to legislate on any topic — public health, morals, and so forth — while the new federal government was designed to be of limited function. This is the notion of a "compound republic," as James Madison aptly dubbed it in *Federalist 51:*

> In a single republic, all the power surrendered by the people is submitted to the administration of a single government; and the usurpations are guarded against by a division of the government into distinct and separate departments. In the compound republic of America, the power surrendered by the people is first divided between two distinct governments, and then the portion allotted to each subdivided among distinct and separate departments. Hence a double security arises to the rights of the people. The different governments will control each other, at the same time that each will be controlled by itself.[6]

Specifically, the Constitution contains 17 clauses laying out relatively narrow areas in which Congress is empowered to legislate, and an eighteenth clause that authorizes Congress to pass any laws "necessary and proper" to the fulfillment of the goals of the prior 17 clauses. While these 17 functions are broader than the capabilities of the central government under the Articles of Confederation — in particular in clauses 1 and 3, which give

Congress the authority to tax and to regulate commerce — the scope of congressional power is indeed limited.

It is important to note that Congress is *not* granted the police power traditionally held by states. And the Constitution does *not* empower Congress to make decisions about morality for the American people. Rather, *Congress was granted the authority only to provide a unified front to foreigners in peacetime and especially in war, to facilitate the exchange of goods, people, and communication among states to encourage the prosperity of the nation as a whole, and to fund the limited scope of these efforts.*

The next important guarantor of limited government is the Bill of Rights. Tellingly, one of the leading proponents of the Constitution, Alexander Hamilton, suggested that no such enumeration of rights was needed because the limited nature of the proposed government implied that *all* nonenumerated rights were retained by the people. But the anti-Federalist who wrote under the pseudonym Brutus captured the skepticism of many when he said, "I cannot help suspecting that persons who attempt to persuade people that such reservations [of explicitly guaranteed liberties] were less necessary under this Constitution than under those of the states, are willfully endeavoring to deceive, and to lead you into an absolute state of vassalage."[7]

As a result, James Madison authored and the states ratified a set of 10 amendments immediately following the ratification of the original text of the Constitution. The first 9 amendments guarantee various individual rights, some of which — such as the right to bear arms — are under attack even now, more than two hundred years after the rights were guaranteed to us. The Tenth Amendment is broader, however. *It states that "the powers not delegated to the United States by the Constitution, nor prohibited by it to the states, are reserved to the states respectively, or to the people."*

Now, some believe this amendment doesn't really mean anything. In one Supreme Court case, Justice Harlan Stone wrote that "the amendment states but a truism that all is retained which has not been surrendered."[8] But to suggest that it has no significance is to diminish the Bill of Rights generally and to ignore history. It clearly was Madison's codification of the verbal guarantee offered by Hamilton, and the echoing of a similar provision in the Articles of Confederation. The Tenth Amendment offers concrete proof that the Founders intended for states to play a leading role not only in governing the people but also in defending the rights of their citizens against the powerful and potentially dangerous central government. It stands for the principle that there is a limit to what Washington can and should do.

The "Great Compromise" that emerged from the Philadelphia Convention created proportional representation in the House of Representatives, and equal representation in the Senate.[9] Because any law passed had to be approved by the Senate, this provision increased the influence and defensive capacities of small states, which were more vulnerable to the democratic majority. Senators would be chosen by the state legislatures rather than directly by the people in order to enhance the senators' allegiance to — and the federal government's deference to — the state sovereigns.

Additionally, state legislatures were empowered to determine the time, place, and manner of congressional elections, to set the qualifications for those running for representative office, and to appoint presidential electors. Senators, representing the states, were given a say in the presidential appointments process through "advice and consent." Furthermore, Congress would not be permitted to discriminate among the states through taxes or regulation, and any taxes collected would be apportioned to the states in proportion to their population.

Why States Remain Liberty's Friend

While the national government was intentionally strong when it came to foreign and war powers, its domestic authority was greatly limited, leaving ample room for the states to be the hub of American self-government. By the will of the people, our government exists to guarantee our right to live according to the dictates of our conscience, to chart the direction for our lives, and to join with like-minded people to journey down that path. States are the vehicles by which we are able to do that. States not only matter; they serve as the core of the great American experiment.

States Allow Us to Live with People of Like Mind

The Founders gave us a federal system of government that, if respected, allows people of varying beliefs to live together united as Americans. We agree that there are certain things we must do together as Americans to be a strong nation—the providing of national defense and security being first and foremost—but most problems get better solutions when they are solved at the local level. And in doing so, we can tailor those solutions to our own values and perspectives rather than trying to create national one-size-fits-all policies.

I would no more consider living in Massachusetts than I suspect a great number of folks from Massachusetts would like to live in Texas. We just don't agree on a number of things. They passed state-run health care, they have sanctioned gay marriage, and they elected Ted Kennedy, John Kerry, and Barney Frank repeatedly—even after actually knowing about them and what they believe!

Texans, on the other hand, elect folks like me. You know the type, the kind of guy who goes jogging in the morning, packing a

Ruger .380 with laser sights and loaded with hollow-point bullets, and shoots a coyote that is threatening his daughter's dog. We like that our law-abiding citizens carry guns down here. We also like to limit regulations, keep taxes low, leave marriage between a man and a woman, and let our citizens choose their own health care plan, to name just a few differences.

In an increasingly diverse and growing nation of over 300 million citizens of varying religious, ethnic, and cultural backgrounds, this benefit has only grown in significance and impact since the Founders contemplated and implemented federalism. From marriage to prayer, from zoning laws to tax policy, from our school systems to health care, and everything in between, it is essential to our liberty that we be allowed to live as we see fit through the democratic process at the local and state level.

That is the blessing of federalism and the importance of states in a nation as large as ours. As one pro-states Revolutionary-era politician writing under the pseudonym of Agrippa said, "The idea of an uncompounded republick [with millions of] inhabitants all reduced to the same standards of morals, of habits, and of laws is in itself an absurdity, and contrary to the whole experience of mankind."[10] Just as each individual is unique, so, too, do we come together to form unique communities with differing needs.

States Promote Mobility

In order to find like-minded people, under federalism Americans can exercise true liberty and "vote with their feet"—choose to leave a climate in one state that is incompatible with their beliefs and go to one more to their liking.

I recall the late Lewis Grizzard, a famous southern comedian and former *Atlanta Journal-Constitution* columnist, once saying about folks moving south, "We don't care, come on down, breathe our air, marry our women … but just one thing … please don't tell us how y'all used to do it back in Cleveland. We don't care. If you like it there, Delta's ready when you are."

Now, I joke a bit. We in Texas are proud that so many of our fellow Americans have sought relief from the heavy taxation and burdens of some of our sister states to move to our state in search of a freer, fairer climate in which to conduct business and live their lives. Our doors are open. But keep in mind that there is a reason people want to come here. We are doing something right, and that is making Texas an attractive place. So pardon us if we don't care to "change our ways" to mirror New York, California, or Michigan.

Ultimately, as long as we avoid a one-size-fits-all federal government solution, no American need ever be forced into a mold that does not fit. In a nation of a single rule of law, a frustrated citizen would have no options and would be forced to lead his life under laws he found oppressive. Under federalism, however, this citizen has the opportunity to exercise his liberty by moving to a state where his preferences are better matched. If he prefers not to pay any state income tax whatsoever, for example, he has the option of moving to Alaska, Florida, Nevada, South Dakota, Texas, Washington, or Wyoming.

This mobility puts competitive pressure on states. Policies that undermine progress and the well-being of a state's citizens will not be long-lived. State politicians have an incentive to identify and satisfy resident preferences so that dissatisfied citizens do not leave, taking their tax dollars with them.

States Limit Centralization of Power

Empowering states prevents the accumulation of power in one central government and limits the extent to which the people must be governed by faraway representatives, bureaucrats, and judges who do not share their beliefs. Americans have been steeped ever since the nation's founding in a healthy fear of tyranny and of being governed from afar, as the Founders were being forced to endure a king 3,000 miles away.

Is it not ironic that what we fought against 200-odd years ago is what we allow today, with the consolidation of power in Washington? Americans are forced to live according to the dictates of people they neither elected nor chose, and from thousands of miles away. After all, even the people of a large state like Texas, with 32 members of the House and 2 senators, are unable to prevent the rest of the nation from forcing them to accept whatever an unchecked Congress decides.

This is not how most Americans want to live. I can tell you, the people of Texas do not want to be told by Nancy Pelosi, Dick Durbin, Henry Waxman — or, for that matter, Mitch McConnell, John Boehner, or any other Republican from another state — what to do. And we certainly don't want to place that kind of control in the hands of nameless, faceless, and unelected federal bureaucrats.

The centralization of power in a country as large as the United States necessarily means that the people are largely unable to participate in many of the decisions that are going to affect them. The Founders recognized this truth even when there were only 13 states with approximately 3.9 million people.[11] As Jefferson noted, "What has destroyed liberty and the rights of man in every government which has ever existed under the sun? The generalizing and concentrating all cares and powers into one body."[12]

But consider how much more the people are separated from their representatives today — and how much more dangerous that "generalizing and concentrating" can be. In the First Congress, there were 65 congressmen, each representing an average of 60,000 Americans.[13] Today, there are 435 representatives for an estimated

310 million people, or over 700,000 people per representative. The same growth is true for senators; the two senators from Virginia, for example, have gone from representing approximately 691,000 people to almost 8 million.[14] So today, then, we should be even more vigilant in our effort to bring decision making back to the state and local level.

States Should Be Laboratories of Democracy

As Justice Louis D. Brandeis wrote, "A single courageous state may, if its citizens choose, serve as a laboratory; and try novel social and economic experiments without risk to the rest of the country."[15] This of course relates to each of the reasons offered above, but it's worth noting independently because it strengthens the nation to experiment with ideas.

It is good if certain states can try income taxes, others sales taxes, and still others — like our friends in New Hampshire, God Bless them — neither (putting aside taxes on dividends and interest)! Some states can try charter schools, vouchers, or homeschooling as education alternatives, and we can study the results. Some states can try different sentencing schemes for their criminals — including, yes, the death penalty — and we can determine what effects they have on crime. States can be free to experiment with different ideas to deal with societal concerns and problems, and they can do so at a level closer to the people so that those particular trials can match the morals and beliefs of the people most affected.

A good example of a state laboratory at work is lawsuit reform. At one time, Texas was one of the worst jurisdictions in the nation for abusive litigation, resulting in runaway damages, enriched lawyers, a poor business climate, fewer doctors, and a generally disastrous civil justice system. We were known as a judicial hellhole. But through the hard work of a few dedicated Texans—such as the leaders at Texas Civil Justice League and Texans for Lawsuit Reform—our state has led the nation in reforming our civil justice system. We now have sensible limits to abusive litigation, including $250,000 caps on noneconomic damages for lawsuits against doctors. The result has been the reversal of the stream of doctors leaving Texas and an increase in the number of people moving here to work in medicine. Similarly, Texas has led the nation in enacting commonsense reforms for asbestos litigation; we made sure that damages are awarded only to people who are truly sick from asbestos exposure instead of allowing lawsuit mills to gin up cases for thousands of people who show no evidence of asbestos-related illness.

On the other side of the coin, Massachusetts is free to experiment with state-run health care. If federalism is respected, the people of Massachusetts are free to try it while the rest of the nation sits back and watches to see if they have any success, and whether any success they do have is worth the price of losing liberty to get it. Now, we in Texas are not too excited about the prospect of government-run anything, much less health care, and the federal health care legislation—known to most as Obamacare—is a direct assault on the principle of federalism. And because of it, we are going to fight the federal government's unconstitutional mandate at every turn.

States Encourage Civic Virtue, Independence, and Self-Reliance

Finally, states encourage civic virtue by enabling the people to participate more actively in public affairs, resulting in greater independence and self reliance. To encourage active involvement in self-governing—a right that had recently been won through war—the new Americans needed to be able to participate in the political process in a way that produced immediate and tangible effects. The empowerment of state and local governments encouraged that participation.

As the great student of American democracy Alexis de Tocqueville wrote, "The institutions of a township are to freedom what primary schools are to science; they put it within reach of the people, they make them taste its peaceful employ and habituate them to making use of it. Without the institutions of a township, a nation may give itself a free government, but it does not have the spirit of freedom."[16] The spirit of liberty and the health of democracy depend on public participation and civic virtue. The reason for this is well articulated by constitutional scholar Matthew Spalding in his great book *We Still Hold These Truths* when he writes:

> The purpose of limiting government, assuring rights, and guaranteeing the consent of the governed is to protect a vast realm of human freedom. That freedom creates a great space for the primary institutions of civil society — family, school, church and private associations — to flourish, forming the habits and virtues required for liberty. The American Founders also knew that it was through these institutions, through the enjoyment of family, faith and community life, that man secured, as it says in the Constitution, "the blessings of liberty" — that liberty which is truly a blessing. Moral self-government both precedes and completes political self-government, and thus political freedom. It is in this sense that the primary as well as the culminating first principle of American liberty is self-government.[17]

So, the very essence of America stems from a limited, decentralized government. When we empower Washington at the expense of local control, we rip apart the concept of civic virtue by removing the ability of the citizens to govern themselves.

Slavery, Civil Rights, and Federalism

Any discussion of the need to empower states inevitably brings with it cynical questions about their role in promoting slavery and hindering the civil rights movement. Indeed, many of our ancestors and forebears ignored the words and spirit of the Declaration of Independence and denied basic liberties and humanity to certain people solely because of the color of their skin. These were inexcusable chapters in American history — particularly for the southern states most responsible. These chapters were often defined by some who championed "states' rights," and thus the concept of federalism has been understandably but mistakenly weakened.

But a careful reading of history shows that active, liberty-loving states greatly contributed to the destruction of slavery in America. After all, by 1850, half of the states in America were free states, while half still permitted their citizens to own slaves. A number of those free states offered protections for blacks against the evils of slavery, such as establishing due-process rights for runaway slaves, while some people in some northern states operated the Underground Railroad to offer a path to freedom. This was federalism, or certainly local control, in action.

Unwilling to give up a way of life inexcusably based on an abominable practice, southern states persuaded Congress — the federal government — to pass the Fugitive Slave Act of 1850, which *compelled* citizens of northern states to act against their conscience and help return escaped former slaves into bondage. Meanwhile, the federal Supreme Court got involved, striking down states' personal liberty laws and ruling in *Dred Scott v. Sanford* that federal territories could not be free and that free states were not entitled to offer the rights of citizenship to former slaves.[18] Thus, while the southern states seceded in the name of "states' rights," in many ways it was the northern states whose sovereignty was violated in the run-up to the Civil War.

We can never know what would have happened in the absence of federal involvement because we cannot rewrite history. There was a major divide in the nation, and it is possible that war was inevitable. But once war was upon the nation, it was the steadfast commitment of Abraham Lincoln to preserve the Union, and ultimately his leadership, that led to a victory by the North and emancipation. And the ultimate result is that the people adopted three constitutional amendments—the Thirteenth, Fourteenth, and Fifteenth—abolishing slavery, protecting due process and equal protection of the laws, and prohibiting race as a factor in eligibility for voting, respectively.

Unfortunately, even after a bloody war, the full freedom offered by these amendments took more than a century to be realized. A combination of factors made that true, including both intervention by the Supreme Court and, sadly, opposition by some in the name of states' rights. But it is important to note that, for all the bluster leading up to and during the civil rights movement by some about states' rights, it was the realization of the purpose and intent of those constitutional amendments—a process that both respected federalism *and* the role of the federal government to use explicit constitutional authority to protect fundamental individual rights—that led to equal rights for all. And it is also important that those of us who are committed to liberty through federalism not be held hostage because some people were misguided or evil in their perpetuation of the scourge of racism in the name of states' rights.

As talk-radio host and lawyer Mark Levin described it in *Liberty and Tyranny*:

> For the Conservative, the lesson comes back to man's imperfection. Even good men are capable of bad things. The disgrace of slavery is a disgrace of the human condition — as is all tyranny. Man's institutions, like man himself, are imperfect. They can be used for good or bad, and they have been used for both. Therefore, diffusing authority among many imperfect men — by enumerating federal power, separating power within the federal government, and sharing power with the states — isolates and limits tyranny. Had slavery been affirmed in the Constitution and urged on all states, who knows when and how it would have been abolished.[19]

My belief in the wherewithal of Texas and her fellow states more than in the wisdom of Washington is not merely a knee-jerk reaction to policies we would rather not see institutionalized. This independence is something that was intended by our Founders, has been cultivated across our country, and has allowed millions of Americans to thrive as free people for generations. Our Founders recognized that man not only naturally seeks liberty but also lives productively and happily with others in his community when liberty is upheld and federalism is respected.

3

What Happened to the Founders' Vision?

There are more instances of the abridgment of the freedom of the people by gradual and silent encroachments of those in power than by violent and sudden usurpations.

— JAMES MADISON, SPEECH TO THE VIRGINIA RATIFYING CONVENTION, JUNE 16, 1788[1]

AFTER A TRAGIC EXPLOSION on a deepwater drilling rig in the Gulf of Mexico in April 2010, the resulting oil leak threatened the coastline of Louisiana. My friend Bobby Jindal, the governor of the people of that great state, was working with his team to find ways to deal with the potentially devastating impact that the oil could have on wildlife, beaches, businesses, fishing, tourism, and innumerable other parts of their lives and economy. The governor needed to move quickly and had identified a course of action he felt was best for Louisiana: placing barriers to the incoming oil. But the federal government told him he couldn't do it, and that the state of Louisiana would have to wait for an environmental impact statement to be completed.

Such is the state of federalism today. I see it firsthand in Texas, too. For the years 2010–2011, our budget is just over $180 billion. Of that, 36 percent, or just $65 billion, is money Texans pay in taxes to Washington, and that is sent back with countless strings to tell us how to spend it.[2] It includes money for health care, education, transportation, and countless other domestic programs not mentioned among those 17 clauses enumerating the powers of the central government.

But the problem goes far deeper than that. Prohibition on school prayer, the redefinition of marriage, the nationalization of health care, the proliferation of federal criminal laws, interference with local education, the increased regulation of food—even telling us what kind of lightbulb we can use—there is seemingly no end to the reach of Washington.

What happened to our country? Such policies represent an almost complete abandonment of a limited central government rooted in federalism. How did we get from a world where our liberty is specifically protected by our government to one where the government decides how we shall live?

Some believe that the turning point for Washington empowerment was the Civil War, but the truth is that ever since the dawn of the so-called Progressive movement over a century ago, liberals have used every tool at their disposal—including, notably, the Supreme Court—to wage a gradual war on the Constitution and the American way of life, with very little effective opposition from conservatives. Most often this war has been waged either silently—as far away from the ballot box as possible—or, in times of crisis, when the American people have been at their weakest and willing to trade a pound of liberty for an ounce of perceived security.

How did this happen?

First, we allowed the Supreme Court and its lower courts to assume a role not envisioned for them by the Founders. We allowed them to become policy makers by judicial fiat and to ignore their fundamental job of interpreting the Constitution and the law as given to them instead of reading virtually everything under the sun into narrowly written clauses.

Second, and perhaps most frustrating, the American people mistakenly empowered the federal government during a fit of populist rage in the early twentieth century by giving it an unlimited source of income (the Sixteenth Amendment) and by changing the way senators are elected (the Seventeenth Amendment).

Third, President Franklin Roosevelt's use of the Great Depression to launch his New Deal set the table for the abuse of federal power, and then a myth surrounding the success of the New Deal clouded policymaking and political choices for generations to come.

Fourth, building upon the New Deal, Congress has further abused its power both to regulate commerce and to spend money, most notably during the Great Society and, again, today. It has used these powers as an excuse to regulate anything it wishes and in so doing has spent recklessly and coerced states to do as Congress, in its infinite wisdom, wishes.

These things did not, of course, happen overnight. Rather, there has been a slow march to socialize this country and rob us of our most basic and fundamental right to live free. This march — rooted in the Progressive movement and expanded in modern liberalism — has been punctuated by periods of staggering government growth predicated on the notion that some problems are so big that only Washington can solve them, but only in ways that ignore the words of the Constitution. It is in these moments of crisis that Americans are most susceptible to government overreaching. As the White House chief of staff to President Obama, Rahm Emanuel, said, "You never want a serious crisis to go to waste."[3]

And have you noticed that modern liberals are trying to shift back to the term "Progressive"? They are doing this because they know they have lost the war in defending liberalism. Like used-car salesmen who started selling "pre-owned vehicles," they are now selling progress. Who can be against progress, after all? But it's a fraudulent use of the word, because for the Progressive, progress is marked not by how free you are but by how much government can "do" for you.

The Progressive Era: Remaking the Constitution with the Sixteenth and Seventeenth Amendments

So what about this so-called Progressive Era, and how did it lead to such dramatic empowerment of Washington?

It came on the heels of the industrial boom of the late 1800s, a period of fairly limited national intervention. During that time, men like Andrew Carnegie, John D. Rockefeller, and Cornelius Vanderbilt revolutionized the steel, oil, and transportation industries, opening up the vast expanse of America to its citizens and lowering the cost of commodities for consumers. While government was of course involved, it was due to the wheels of commerce that patent applications exploded, hundreds of thousands of miles of rail lines were added, electricity grids became increasingly widespread, corporations were developed — all while literally millions of immigrants flocked to America, laying the foundation for our modern, ethnically diverse workforce.

Roughly contemporaneously with the growth of industrialization, the Progressive movement developed, reflecting a desire both to contain the new national growth and to make sure the benefits were shared by all. Progressives saw the increasing industrialization and modernization of America as a change so great that it required a rethinking of the way the government worked. Gone, they said, were the days of Jeffersonian agrarianism, when self-employed farmers around the country were capable of providing for themselves.

Now that more Americans were working in factories and mills and living closer and closer together, the Progressives believed that the era of "live and let live" was obsolete. The new attitude of a national government inspired and dominated by Progressive thought was best summed up by President Woodrow Wilson:

> We used to think in the old-fashioned days when life was very simple that all that government had to do was to put on a policeman's uniform, and say, "Now don't anybody hurt anybody else." We used to say that the ideal of government was for every man to be left alone and not interfered with, except when he interfered with somebody else; and that the best government was the government that did as little governing as possible. That was the idea that obtained in Jefferson's time. But we are coming now to realize that life is so complicated that we are not dealing with the old conditions, and that the law has to step in and create new conditions under which we may live, the conditions which will make it tolerable for us to live.[4]

This view — that government should be an interventionist force in American society — remains alive and well today. It grew out of this era, when politicians began arguing that Americans could not control the circumstances of their lives, so government had to be an equalizing force. To me, the idea of living under a distant government that dictates those circumstances and what I may and may not do is not comforting but intolerable. But that is the ethos of the Progressives. Their idea of change is to exploit fear in order to exercise greater control rather than watching to see where the American imagination takes us.

Much of the Progressive movement, though, was simply a reaction to perceived, and sometimes real, excesses of the Gilded Age and represented the first attempts to, as Barack Obama likes to say, "spread the wealth around." Of course, the obvious point is that these industrialists created millions of jobs and massive opportunity for millions more, literally building the infrastructure upon which the world's greatest economy would grow. But having earned more from their innovations and business strategies in contemporary terms than Warren Buffett or Bill Gates has, they also redefined the concept of American philanthropy, each of them donating staggering funds to charity.

Consider that Carnegie gave away at least $370 million,[5] and Rockefeller roughly $537 million — both of which in today's dollars would translate into donations of hundreds of billions of dollars.[6] Because this much wealth was almost unimaginable — which the men themselves clearly recognized, given the generous ways they charitably disposed of it — and because it was so concentrated, Progressives saw an opportunity to get their hands on that money to spend it in ways *they* thought best.

This leads me to the great milestone on the road to serfdom: the passage of the Sixteenth Amendment. It gave Congress the authority to levy an income tax on American citizens and absolved the federal government from a previous requirement that any such taxes be returned to states proportionally to their collection. This was the birth of wealth redistribution in the United States. It created a giant faucet of money for the federal government and ensured that state cooperation in federal programs would not be necessary for Washington to enact whatever expensive laws it saw fit to administer.

But why, you might ask, would states ratify an amendment that gives the federal government direct access to our wallets while relinquishing state control over what happens with the money taken? According to historian John Buenker, the simple answer seems to be that it was the combination of a populist view that existing tax structures didn't touch enough of the Gilded Age wealth and a belief that the new tax would never touch the lower and middle classes. Buenker writes that "the claim that 'only the rich will pay' was heard in state legislatures across the land" as the Sixteenth Amendment was being ratified.[7]

Oops. "We the people" messed up. Or we were snookered. Either way, we forgot how important it is to guard against the centralization of power, and that when you give the federal government an inch, it takes a mile. What was promised to be a tax that would affect only the wealthiest 3 to 5 percent of Americans is now paid by roughly half of the population.[8] And while marginal tax rates ranged from 1 to 7 percent right after the amendment was ratified, today rates range from 10 to 35 percent (for now) and have been as high as 70 to 90 percent of income over the years.[9] This is on top of entitlement taxes of more than 12 percent. So today the federal income tax produces well over $1 trillion in revenue for the federal government to spend on thousands of programs.[10]

But the Progressives were not finished. They dealt another blow to the ability of states to exert influence on the federal government with the passage and ratification of the Seventeenth Amendment. That amendment established the direct election of senators, replacing the constitutionally prescribed system of state legislatures choosing them. The Founders, of course, set it up that way on purpose. As noted on the Senate website, "The state legislatures, they argued, would provide the necessary 'filtration' to produce better senators — the elect of the elected. The framers hoped that this arrangement would give state political leaders a sense of participation, calming their fears about the dangers of a strong centralized government."[11]

The two practical reasons for the change were corruption in local elections and the fact that when a state legislature deadlocked on its senatorial election, the state went unrepresented in Washington. But that problem was only an opportunity for the Progressives. Well-known Progressive William Randolph Hearst used his publishing empire to promote the Seventeenth Amendment in a series of muckraking articles. Favoring centralization, Progressives saw this as a way for Americans to increasingly identify with the national government and give up their parochial local interests.

With the passage of the Sixteenth and Seventeenth Amendments, states handed over significant chunks of their sovereignty and wealth to the federal government. Congress was free to tax and spend to its heart's content—and with little accountability. Now Congress had a big pot of money, and with the proportionality requirement for taxation gone and with senators now being elected by the people, there was significant political incentive to spend as much as possible. Indeed, with this newfound source of money, the term "pork barrel" spending gained increased notoriety.[12] If higher taxes were required (of others), then so be it. The states, and the people, had traded structural difficulties and some local corruption for a much larger and dangerous form of corruption.

The New Deal Sets the Stage for a Massive Federal Government

There was one hitch left for the Progressives. The Constitution limited the power of Congress. It could not, for example, make laws regarding manufacturing, unions, or minimum wages, because those activities occurred within the boundaries of states and were not part of the interstate commerce that the Constitution authorized Congress to regulate. As the Supreme Court said in 1918, "The power of the states to regulate their purely internal affairs by such laws as seem wise to the local authority is inherent and has never been surrendered to the [national] government."[13]

And yet, today, the national government runs rampant through states' "purely internal affairs." What happened? What happened was the New Deal—when an arrogant President Roosevelt and an emboldened Congress saw the opportunity to use a crisis to expand Washington's influence, and the Supreme Court let them do it by abdicating its role as the protector of constitutional federalism.

This era represents the second big step in the march of socialism and was the key to releasing the remaining constraints on the national government's power to do whatever it wishes. In probably the greatest power grab in American history—and triggered by a crisis Rahm Emanuel would have loved—FDR tried to change the way that citizens interacted with their government. In particular, he positioned business as an enemy of the people, and government as their savior. This allowed government to dictate not only the price of goods but which goods consumers would be allowed to buy.

Forming the first ingredients for today's federal alphabet soup, the country was given the AAA, the CCC, the FERA, the RFC, the NIRA, the SEC, the PWA, the TVA, and more. Now, I could tell you what each stood for, but do you care? Undemocratic, unelected Washington bureaucrats were now (dubiously) empowered to dictate their own preferences to the American people.

The two most radical of these acts were the National Industrial Recovery Act and the Agricultural Adjustment Act—so radical, in fact, that the Supreme Court ruled each unconstitutional almost immediately. The NIRA forced industries to establish "codes" dictating how goods could be manufactured—from wages and hours regulations to "the precise components of macaroni"—and how much a merchant could charge for them.[14] The AAA, similarly, was designed to prop up the price of agricultural goods, essentially by paying farmers to farm less or simply by mandating that they destroy their crops (or livestock) and that they refrain from growing food for their own consumption.

For the first half of the 1930s, the Supreme Court was resolute in fighting against this power grab. In the landmark *Schechter Poultry* case in 1935, the Court struck down the NIRA, saying, "Extraordinary conditions may call for extraordinary remedies. But the argument necessarily stops short of an attempt to justify action which lies outside the sphere of constitutional authority. Extraordinary conditions do not create or enlarge constitutional power."[15] The opinion continued, "The authority of the federal government may not be pushed to such an extreme as to destroy the distinction, which the Commerce Clause itself establishes, between commerce 'among the several States' and the internal concerns of a State."

Now, please do not get me wrong here. I am loath to look to the Supreme Court to protect us. In fact, the Court often contributed to the very federal power grab it was invalidating, when it struck down state laws that sought to enact similar policies—such as state minimum-wage laws, limits on hours worked, and so on. But the Court should and did defend the Constitution against the federal government's encroachment on the sovereignty of the states in these instances.

All that changed in 1937, when the Court gave a new meaning to the Commerce Clause. For whatever reasons—politics, timing, a change of heart, or FDR's threat to "pack the court" with more liberal justices—the Court ignored recent precedent and ruled that another of Roosevelt's initiatives, the National Labor Relations Act, was constitutional because "it is the effect upon commerce, not the source of the injury, which is the criterion."[16] State boundaries, it seemed, were no longer relevant. Five years later, the Court took this "effect on commerce" rationale to an absurd extreme, finding that the federal government could prohibit a man from growing wheat *on his own property for his own consumption* because if that effect were aggregated, it might have a negative impact on the national price of wheat.[17]

And since that opinion in the heart of the New Deal, the national government has been largely free to expand its powers with utter disregard for the sovereignty expressly retained by the states. The states had been cast aside in the face of this vast intrusion into realms in which, traditionally, they were the sole sovereigns *and* in which they had either chosen not to legislate or had already chosen their preferred policy.

But to what end?

The Myth of the New Deal and Its Dubious Legacy

If the New Deal had not effectively been a complete and total failure, perhaps it would be funny. But, the sad reality is that a romanticized and rose-tinted view promoted by liberal scholars and passed down for generations has created a legend that has long been relied upon for unlimited expansion of the federal government.

I say that as a reformed New Deal Democrat. I grew up on a cotton farm in West Texas. My parents were New Deal Democrats, so I was a New Deal Democrat, too. Don't get me wrong, we were God-fearing conservatives who believed that there is right and wrong and that family values matter. We were taught about fundamental American principles of self-reliance and personal responsibility, as well as taking care of our families and our communities. But we were also taught as children that, in the words of the Alabama song, "the cotton was short and the weeds were tall, but Mr. Roosevelt's a gonna save us all."[18]

That was the "Song of the South," after all—that it was the

New Deal that had saved us from the depths of the Depression and the Dust Bowl. As one syndicated columnist, Mona Charen, put it:

> You know the fairy tale. You were probably taught it in school. During the 1920s, America practiced laissez-faire economics. The 1920s were seen, as historian Amity Shlaes put it, as a period of "false growth and low morals." Greedy businessmen got out of control and created a market crash in 1929. President Hoover, obedient to Republican ideas concerning noninterference in the market, did nothing. The economy spiraled into a depression. Roosevelt was elected in 1932, banished fear, inaugurated the New Deal, and put America back to work.[19]

But the whole thing was a fraud and simply does not stand up to history. I recognized that in the 1980s after watching President Ronald Reagan institute market reforms to truly get us out of an economic mess, and I became a Republican. Now I am happy to see courageous writers such as Ms. Shlaes in *The Forgotten Man* and Burton Folsom in *New Deal or Raw Deal?* bring to light just what a myth the successes of the New Deal truly are.

Consider that when FDR took office in 1933, unemployment was at 25 percent. It still topped 20 percent six years later, in 1939.[20] The country experienced another "depression within the depression" in 1938, which economist Milton Friedman has observed was "the only occasion in our record when one deep depression followed immediately on the heels of another."[21] Economist Lester Chandler noted that while the Depression was an international event, it was deeper and more prolonged in the United States.[22] But did not FDR do everything he could to stimulate the economy? The mantra, after all, was "Relief, Reform, Recovery."

Well, Henry Morgenthau, Jr., FDR's longtime friend and treasury secretary, said to Democrats on the Ways and Means Committee in May 1939:

> We have tried spending money. We are spending more than we have ever spent before and it does not work. And I have just one interest...I want to see this country prosperous. I want to see people get a job. I want to see people get enough to eat. We have never made good on our promises....I say after eight years of this administration we have just as much unemployment as when we started....And an enormous debt to boot![23]

Recovery did not come until World War II, when FDR was finally persuaded to unleash private enterprise.

And there you have it: the vaunted New Deal did not bring the country out of the Great Depression, but the bigger problem now is that its numerous programs never died, and like a bad disease, they have spread. The impact of the New Deal is staggering not just because of the number of programs but also because of their scope. Certain of these programs massively altered the relationship between Americans and their government with respect to critical aspect of our lives, violently tossing aside any respect for our founding principles of federalism and limited government.

By far the best example of this is Social Security. A New Deal invention, it was clearly intended to be a permanent fixture of the entitlement state FDR was constructing. Private pensions were largely solvent and performing, despite the Depression. Even though the Social Security Act was passed in 1935, the fact that no retirement benefits would be paid until 1942 contradicts any notion that it was directed at an emergency. Moreover, retirement benefits were not payable until age 62, when the life expectancy at the time was only 60.[24] And FDR beat back a popular proposal for a private option. Apparently FDR agreed with Progressive senator Robert M. La Follette, who explained why Washington should not give people a choice:

> If we shall adopt this [private option], the government having determined to set up a federal system of old-age insurance will provide, in its own bill creating that system, competition which in the end may destroy the federal system.... It would be inviting and encouraging competition with its own plan which ultimately would undermine and destroy it.[25]

FDR was aware that Social Security would not be good for the job market, when jobs were what Americans needed most. He had to admit that the payroll taxes used to fund the program would lead to further unemployment by increasing the costs of hiring a worker. "'I guess you're right on the economics,' he said, 'but those [payroll] taxes were never a problem of economics. They are political all the way through.... With those taxes in there, no damn politician can ever scrap my social security program.'"[26] And this was just the beginning, as Arthur Altmeyer, chairman of the board charged with administering Social Security, noted:

> Passing the law is only...the "curtain raiser" in the evolution of such a program. It is already possible to distinguish at least three phases of this evolution...first, the double-barreled job of setting up administrative machinery and of getting it into operation; second, the development and integration of administration and services within the present framework; and third, further expansion to liberalize existing provisions.[27]

In 1939, not even five years later, the program was expanded to provide dependents' and survivors' benefits, and to begin monthly payments in 1940, two years earlier than originally planned.[28] Of course, payroll taxes have increased substantially as well over the decades, starting at 2 percent but standing now at more than 12 percent.

Social Security is something we have been forced to accept for more than 70 years now. Because of that, as Nobel laureate economist Milton Friedman wrote, the program "is one of those things on which the tyranny of the status quo is beginning to work its magic. Despite the controversy that surrounded its inception, it has come to be so much taken for granted that its desirability is hardly questioned any longer."[29]

And there stands a crumbling monument to the failure of the New Deal, in stark contrast to the mythical notion of salvation to which it has wrongly been attached for too long, all at the expense of respect for the Constitution and limited government.

On the Back of the New Deal, Washington Knows No Limits

So why model the expansion of Washington on a failed set of ideas like the New Deal, anyway? Because once politicians taste power, like an alcoholic they gulp it down and seek more. And this is the fourth reason we have ended up where we are today. Recognizing that Americans won't stand for an open attack on their way of life, greedy politicians have worked over time, program by program and inch by inch, to exceed their enumerated powers. Since the New Deal, Congress, presidents, and bureaucrats have taken the ball and run with it, abusing predominantly the Commerce Clause and the spending power, as they are often called, to accomplish their statist objectives. And this abuse has been far from trivial.

The Commerce Clause

The Commerce Clause to which I have alluded several times is one of the 17 enumerated powers found in Article 1, Section 8, of the Constitution, and it grants Congress the power to "regulate commerce...among the several states." Through it, Congress has written laws covering a vast array of subjects. Consider that it is this clause that forms the basis for federal laws regulating the environment, regulating guns, protecting civil rights, establishing the massive programs of Medicare and Medicaid, creating national minimum-wage laws, establishing national labor laws—the list goes on and on.

Now let me preempt the naysayers out there who want to paint me as a backwards southern governor or some other nonsense simply because I believe in federalism and a limit to national power. Let me preempt the genius reporter who will seek to "catch" me with a supernovel question like "So, Governor Perry, you've written a book about states' rights and now complain about abuse of the Commerce Clause. You don't think the Civil Rights Act should have been passed, then, huh?"

Wrong. The Civil Rights Act, which, among many things, prohibited private discrimination in so-called public accommodations, such as hotels and restaurants, was the glorious fulfillment of the principles of the Declaration of Independence and, ultimately, the intent behind passage of the Reconstruction Era amendments. I believe there was ample basis for the establishment of that law in that following the Civil War the people ratified three amendments, the purpose of which was to give the federal government the power to fight racial discrimination. That the Commerce Clause was used in the 1960s to reverse the course the Supreme Court took in 1883 when it ruled the original (and similar) Civil Rights Act of 1875 unconstitutional—notwithstanding the fact that the Act was passed by virtually the same Congress that passed the Fourteenth Amendment, upon which it was based — is not the issue to me. As a legal matter, racial discrimination of that sort arguably affected interstate commerce.

But I am concerned about two things. First is the nonsensical idea that somehow the use of the Commerce Clause as a basis for the Civil Rights Act means that anything goes now — such as nationalized health care — and that if someone opposes that misguided notion, he must also have opposed the Civil Rights Act. Second, I am concerned that we are basing the nationalization of significant aspects of our lives on the Commerce Clause, when doing so weakens the Constitution. Surely we can do better than using a single clause designed to regulate commerce to justify something as significant as prohibiting racial discrimination or ensuring that we have clean air and water.

The Court has further buttressed unfettered use of the Commerce Clause by applying what it calls "minimum rationality review" to such cases. In laymen's speak, that means that if there is any conceivable relation between the regulation of an activity and interstate commerce — even if Congress has not taken the trouble to identify that relation — then the Court will defer to Congress's authority to regulate. Voilà! Congress can do anything it wants.

To be fair, in the 1990s, there was a brief, glorious retreat from the previous 60 years of the Court's allowing unfettered discretion by the federal government to legislate anything it wanted under commerce. The Court, for example, found that a handful of activities were simply too far removed from commerce to be federally regulated, such as gun ownership near schools and the battering of women.[30] The Court also found unconstitutional the federal government's "compel[led] enlistment" of state employees in carrying out federal policies, one of the more powerful antistatist doctrines now available.[31] But the trend was short-lived. The

Court subsequently ruled that Congress, using its Commerce Clause power, could prevent California from legalizing medicinal marijuana.[32] In other words, the federal government has the full prerogative to intervene in your private home if you are engaged in any activity that has some minimal relationship to the exchange of goods.

The Spending Power

Paralleling this expansion in Commerce Clause power was an expansion of the scope of the taxing and spending power. As one anti-Federalist presciently said, "The authority to lay and collect taxes is the most important of any power that can be granted; it connects with it almost all other powers, or at least will in process of time draw all others after it."[33]

As with the Commerce Clause power, the Court initially found that, while the spending power was not limited by the explicitly enumerated powers of Congress, it was nevertheless not broad enough to "invade the reserved rights of the states."[34] In other words, what the federal government could not achieve through its explicit or implied powers, it could not induce the states or citizens of the states to do through bribery. Not one year after the Court had reaffirmed this sovereign sphere of the states — now, once again, in that fateful New Deal year of 1937 — the Justices reversed themselves, calling the states merely "quasi-sovereign" and finding that financial inducements were not equivalent to coercion.[35]

A modern example of this is the bribery of states to maintain their drinking ages at 21. The federal government cannot itself set state drinking ages because — somehow — this has managed to escape the grasp of the Commerce Clause. Instead, Washington threatens to withhold federal highway funds unless the state passes its own law to the specifications set by Washington. This, the Court continues to say, is valid.[36] So it goes with state seat belt laws, the implementation of education policies and standards, and countless other examples.

Are we, as states, complicit in this? I suppose so, in that from time to time we have valued the money more than our sovereignty. But it is a no-win situation: ignore the tremendous transportation needs of a growing state like Texas and you get painted as an impractical ideologue; take the money and you no longer care about principle. Politically, it is hard for state politicians to refuse such funds — particularly when it came right out of the pockets of their constituents in the first place. You can see the box Washington puts us in. This is something I know a little about.

Beyond this practical frustration, though, lies the philosophical problem behind this practice. As University of Texas scholar Lynn Baker points out, conditional spending enables "an end run around the federal amendment procedure. It [offers] a simple majority of Congress the option of denying states a power reserved to them under the Tenth Amendment...without the burden of securing a federal constitutional amendment to that effect."[37]

So how'd it happen? How did we get here when our country was set up thoughtfully, with a government that was limited at the federal level and strong at the state and local level? The New Deal and the explosion of government intervention that accompanied it marked the decline from federalism to statism and the beginning of the rise of the giant welfare state. Aside from those pitifully few doors that remained closed to national regulation, the federal government had become one of plenary power, free to foist political agendas upon the American citizenry with no regard to the Constitution.

If it wasn't already obvious, the fact that the New Deal had truly transformed the way Americans conducted government became clear by the 1960s, during Lyndon Johnson's Great Society. Demonstrating that the national government was no longer constrained by any notions of enumeration, Johnson's Great Society legislation identified and sought to "remedy" areas throughout American life that displeased the statist. From housing to public television, from the environment to art, from education to medical care, from public transportation to food, and beyond, Washington took greater control of powers that were conspicuously missing from Article 1 of the Constitution. Johnson achieved the passage of over 200 major pieces of legislation and created countless new departments. And today we stand on the precipice of doing it again.

In the wake of the New Deal, we have allowed Progressives to successfully frame the debate. Republicans constantly allow themselves to be trapped into thinking they are against people if they oppose certain programs. So instead of fighting the tough fight and articulating their opposition, they too often acquiesce for fear of seeming heartless.

But there is something more to it — something that affects people of both parties. Few people have the discipline to restrain themselves, but politicians tend to have a particular lust for power. And once they have obtained it, they naturally set out to expand it. While it is the disease of members of both parties, it is most acute among Progressives, who feel no guilt or shame in consolidating all power in Washington. They actually believe that they know what is best for all of us, so it is second nature for them to acquire and consolidate power. Unfortunately, this comes at our expense, in the form of the demise of federalism and the loss of liberty. They fuel their movement on fear and misinformation and prey on the American people at times of crisis. Times such as today.

4

Washington Is Bankrupting America

*If you put the federal government in charge of the
Sahara Desert, in five years there'd be a shortage of sand.*

— ANONYMOUS

EMPOWERED BY THE BRAZEN abandonment of limited
government under the New Deal and subsequent regimes, from
the Great Society to the current administration, Washington is
steering America down a path to destruction. The size and scope
of the national government have exploded, and it is on the verge
of becoming *too big to save*. While politicians refuse to discuss this
issue, unless we reverse course, the government bonanza will soon
cripple our country.

In short, Washington is bankrupting America. The amount of
government spending occurring today is staggering, and we are
seeing literally only the tip of a *Titanic*-sized iceberg looming on
the horizon. The amount of money involved is so great that it is
too overwhelming to comprehend.

The national debt is already more than $13.4 trillion.[1] For per-
spective, that is over $43,000 per man, woman, and child in

America. Worse yet, the debt is growing by more than $4 billion a day.[2] This year alone, the federal government will spend a staggering $3.7 trillion, an increase in annual spending of more than $1.4 trillion since just one decade ago.[3] Our total debt is more than twice the economy of every nation on earth except our own, and we are fast approaching as much debt as our gross domestic product (GDP) of just over $14 trillion.

Now, debt in and of itself is not necessarily a problem. Responsibly used and managed, borrowed money is a useful tool. But the financial obligations our country is confronting are anything but manageable, and we may well be facing a "perfect storm" of too much debt, low-growth economic policies, rising interest rates, and the final realization of the true cost of the welfare state. The most alarming problem is that we have no national leadership that will acknowledge this fact and do something about it.

Consider that at only one time in our country's history has the national debt surpassed 100 percent of our economy, or GDP. It was 1945–1947, at the close of World War II, when all national resources were tapped to defeat evil in the form of Imperial Japan and Nazi Germany.[4] Yet today, we stand at just over a 90 percent ratio of debt to GDP. And while we are now at war against radical Islamic terrorists who wage jihad on innocent civilians around the globe, the war is hardly causing today's obscene levels of debt. Consider that in 1945 defense spending was 37.5 percent of GDP. That is an extraordinary amount of money relative to the economic output of our nation at the time. Today, however, defense spending, even while we are at war, is only about 4.8 percent of GDP.[5]

Interestingly, Admiral Michael Mullen, chairman of the Joint Chiefs of Staff, commented that the biggest national security threat we face as a country is not the Taliban or Al-Qaeda, but the debt.[6] A Gallup poll asked Americans what they perceived to be the most worrisome threat to the United States, and the debt tied with terrorism for number one.[7] Americans see the debt as a more acute threat than the wars in Iraq and Afghanistan.

Our ability to handle $13.2 trillion of debt and counting is far less certain than what we dealt with after World War II when hundreds of thousands of GIs returned home and kickstarted the baby boom. Unencumbered by a welfare state still in its infancy, America then enjoyed steady and strong economic growth that allowed us to move beyond our debt (that is, we grew our economy faster than debt to get to a point where it was manageable).

Today we have a much different situation. First, the culmination of seventy years of entitlements—from Social Security and unemployment insurance to Medicare and Medicaid—is now upon us. The bill is due, and we can't afford it. Second, today's unprincipled politicians have developed and embraced a culture of reckless, wasteful spending, where earmarks and unnecessary, unconstitutional programs are the norm and continue to explode out of control. Third, and finally, the economic impacts of the policies of the Obama administration, combined with the burdens of failed New Deal and other legacy policies that created the modern administrative state, are crippling growth as opposed to encouraging it, as seen in the specters of higher taxes, so-called stimulus spending, massive amounts of regulation, and a reprise of New Deal–type programs like Obamacare.

Runaway Entitlement Spending

By far the most alarming problem we face with respect to the largesse of the federal government is the very real crisis of the looming implosion of New Deal and Great Society entitlement programs. Consider that federal expenditures for 2010 include more than $721 billion for Social Security, $457 billion for Medicare, and $284 bil-

lion for Medicaid and the Children's Health Insurance Program —
up 38 percent, 81 percent, and 87 percent, respectively, since a decade
ago.[8] But those numbers are hard to understand out of context.

In 2010, federal spending of $741 billion for Health and Human
Services (which includes Medicare, Medicaid, and CHIP) and $721
billion for Social Security each accounted for a *larger* part of our
budget than our wartime defense spending of approximately $719
billion. Add welfare payments for unemployment and other income-
security programs of about $557 billion, interest on the national debt
of almost $188 billion, and the "mandatory" spending before our
legislators even start working, for a grand total of just over $2.2 tril-
lion.[9] This represents about 60 percent of the $3.7 trillion we spent in
2010, which left us with a single-year deficit of $1.5 trillion.[10]

These numbers tell the alarming story of Washington largesse
better than any words I can assemble, and I am afraid it gets
much, much worse. Because Social Security, Medicare, and Medicaid grow automatically as more citizens become eligible for benefits, they will continue to eat up progressively more of the overall
budget. Just ten years from now in 2020, these three entitlement
programs, along with interest on the debt, will cost a combined
$3.5 trillion,[11] almost equal to the entire federal budget for 2010!
Indeed, even accounting for projected growth in our economy, a
tax increase of $12,000 per household will be required to pay for
the three programs by 2050.[12]

Worried yet? Well, it actually gets more astounding. On top of
our national debt of $13.2 trillion and climbing, and on top of
numerous other liabilities (including state debt and pension
funds — state legislatures and governors do not have entirely clean
hands either), the combined liabilities for Social Security and
Medicare amount to $106 trillion.[13] That number is so absurdly
large that it's incomprehensible. Unfortunately, we have precisely
$0 in the bank to pay these liabilities.

Aren't you wondering about the Social Security Trust Fund you've heard so much about? Well, it must be somewhere in Al Gore's lockbox, right next to his notes from inventing the Internet and that global cooling data he doesn't want anyone to see. The term "trust fund" leads one to believe that there is a stockpile of assets that can be drawn on to pay benefits. Not so. This trust fund is an elaborate illusion cooked up by government magicians.

Social Security is a pay-as-you-go system, meaning that current payroll taxes are used to fund benefits. Any extra revenues have funded general government obligations for generations in return for IOUs from the U.S. Treasury.[14] Thus, it is a ruse for politicians to tell us not to worry, because there's $2.4 trillion in the Social Security Trust Fund.[15] While it is true that there is an accumulated *accounting* surplus in this amount, the surplus exists only in a "bookkeeping sense," as the Office of Management and Budget admitted in 2000.[16] Washington has already blown the money. You can think of it as an IOU that we're all going to have to pay.

Kevin Williamson summed up the situation in an article in the *National Review:*

> Suffice it to say, we're a bit short of that $106 trillion. In fact, we're exactly $106 trillion short, since the total value of the Social Security "trust fund" is less than the value of the change you've got rattling around behind your couch cushions, its precise worth being: $0.00. Because the "trust fund" (which is not a trust fund) is by law "invested" (meaning, not invested) in Treasury bonds, there is no national nest egg to fund these entitlements....Seeing no political incentives to reduce benefits, [Bruce] Bartlett calculates that an 81 percent tax increase will be necessary to pay those obligations. "Those who think otherwise are either grossly ignorant of the fiscal facts, in denial, or living in a fantasy world."[17]

The really bad news is that Social Security has finally reached its tipping point. No more free lunch. For the first time, the program will pay out more in benefits than it collects in taxes for the year, and this is just the beginning.[18] So, keeping in mind that there really is no trust fund, this means that our debt will increase all the faster as we pay out more than we take in.

For too long, politicians afraid to face hard facts have been patching Social Security together with Band-Aids. They have been making fraudulent promises to the American people in order to perpetuate their own political careers, and now the chickens are coming home to roost, as the saying goes. An aging population with large numbers of retirees now wants to cash in on those promises.

Ponzi schemes—like the one that sent Bernard Madoff to prison—are illegal in this country for a reason. They are fraudulent systems designed to take in a lot of money at the front and pay out none in the end. This unsustainable fiscal insanity is the true legacy of Social Security and the New Deal. Deceptive accounting has hoodwinked the American public into thinking that Social Security is a retirement system and financially sound, when clearly it is not.

If only the New Dealers had been kind enough to allow workers to make their own choice about whether to participate. As we know from experience, individuals would have done better on their own. Indeed, many private pension plans return 8 percent per year, compared to Social Security's paltry 2 percent or less.[19] Also, before the government padlocked the door in 1983, municipal governments were allowed to opt out of the system. Fittingly, three Texas counties—Galveston, Matagorda, and Brazoria—did so. In 1981, Galveston county employees, for example, voted 78 percent to 22 percent to leave Social Security for a private option.[20] Employees in those private plans, having exercised their liberty at Washington's sufferance, are reaping the benefits.[21]

By any measure, Social Security is a failure. As author Jim Powell points out in *FDR's Folly,* one pro-FDR historian justified Social Security not on its merits but as an important "symbolic gesture to demonstrate that Roosevelt's heart was in the right place."[22] This sounds a lot like justifying the current administration's policies because well-meaning politicians want to provide "hope."

Now, if you say Social Security is a failure, as I have just done, you will inherit the wind of political scorn. Seniors might think you want to cut the benefits they have paid for. Politicians will seek to take advantage, stirring up fear about benefits that will be lost if you elect another "heartless Republican." I get it. That's why only retired senators chair entitlement commissions.

We are told that no politician has the courage to raise these issues, even if avoiding them puts us on the fast track to financial ruin. But by remaining quiet, politicians are really saying they think the American people won't understand it if we share the grim details of our financial future, and that voters will simply kill—or vote against—the messenger in order to continue to receive an underfunded benefit that robbed them of the tens of thousands of dollars they should have made.

Is that how we should respect our fellow citizens? By underestimating their intelligence, their desire to retire with greater stability, or their commitment to the next generation? Programs and attitudes like this show just how much the New Deal tossed away. A new culture of do-something-itis now trumps any constitutional restraint and feeds the political beast in Washington, and each generation of national politicians wants to make its mark by finding another place to expand government, failing to truly address the problems created by the previous generation's expansion of government. And this brings me to the second concern I have about managing our growing debt.

A Culture of Reckless Spending

Although the debt has been at dangerous levels for years now, Washington has not only ignored the problem, it has made it worse. Both Democrats and Republicans share the blame, from President Lyndon B. Johnson, who implemented his inaptly named Great Society, which gave us Medicare and Medicaid (among other programs), to my friend President George W. Bush, who signed into law large education increases and a massive expansion of Medicare to the tune of more than $500 billion for prescription drugs.[23] And it was clear that Republicans in Wash ington lost their way when their arguments revolved around how large the drug benefit should be and not whether funding it was the proper role for taxpayers to play.

To be fair, the Democrats' only complaint about Bush's increases on these programs and others was that they were not enough. They wanted the prescription drug bill to cost twice as much and encouraged more spending on education, health research, and veterans' benefits. The Democrats did not get their way, but since 2000, antipoverty spending is still up 89 percent, and elementary and secondary education spending is up 219 percent.[24]

These examples of large programs—and others like them—are rooted in an irresponsible culture of spending in Washington that has eliminated any sense of the ordinary. No one can run a house or a family budget the way Washington runs our nation's. Washington politicians have so little concern for how money is being spent that they might as well be using Monopoly money. They see no problem with spending other people's money for pork projects in their district or state. They see no problem with spending other people's money for the next feel-good program that a lobbyist brings to them. They see no problem with making appropriations legislation so complicated, long, and last-minute that it is impossible for anyone — citizen or legislator — to know what's in it. There simply are no limits.

Earmarks represent the wasteful spending that has most caught public interest of late and for good reason. While earmarks have been prevalent since the Sixteenth Amendment opened the spigots of cash for Congress, they have never been as out of control as they are today. Consider that President Reagan vetoed a 1987 transportation bill because it had 152 pork projects in it (which Congress promptly overrode),[25] and that in 1991 there were only 546 earmarks requested worth $3.2 billion.[26] Yet in 2010, there were 9,129 earmarks accounting for $16.5 billion. The good news, if there is any, is that this is down from 10,160 projects worth $19.6 billion in 2009, and a peak cost of $29 billion under Republican control in 2006.[27]

Why do we care about $29 billion in earmarks when our national deficit this year will be around $1.5 trillion? Because earmarks corrupt the process and divert attention from the real task of governing and oversight.[28] Besides, if you can't get that right, how in the world can you be trusted to figure out the massive mess that is Social Security or health care? The answer is that you can't. Senator Tom Coburn (R-OK) has aptly called earmarks, or pork-barrel spending, the "gateway drug" to spending addiction. He is right — and he explained it quite effectively in a March 2008 statement regarding a vote on an amendment for a modest one-year moratorium on earmarks:

In addition to being an unconstitutional perversion of our duties, earmarks also drive spending higher and distract Congress from its oversight responsibilities. Earmarks are the gateway drug to spending addiction in Congress because they encourage members of Congress to vote for bloated bills they would otherwise oppose. Earmarks also waste money outright, contrary to the views of many members. If Congress stopped earmarking we could reduce spending by the same amount. We are not helpless victims to the budget rules we set for ourselves. Plus, the effective legislator is not one who sends money back to his or her state through pork. Instead, the effective legislator is one who prevents money from leaving their state.[29]

The amendment, of course, was defeated 29–71. However, due to pressure from the Tea Party movement and an extremely frustrated American public, the idea of a moratorium remains alive, and at least the House GOP voted as a conference in March of 2010 to adopt a moratorium. What legislators should do is adopt a moratorium on pork until the budget is actually balanced, but don't hold your breath. In fact, the GOP failed to mention earmarks in its "agenda" document released in the fall of 2010.

Ultimately, earmarks are indeed just a gateway. Consider whether you believe any of the following is an appropriate and good way to spend taxpayer money, earmark or otherwise:[30]

- Government auditors spent the past five years examining all federal programs and found that 22 percent of them — costing taxpayers a total of $123 billion annually — fail to show any positive impact on the populations they serve.
- Washington spends $25 billion annually maintaining unused or vacant federal properties.
- Washington will spend $615,175 on an archive honoring the Grateful Dead.
- Each month, taxpayers provide $40,000 worth of office space, cell phones, staff, and an SUV for former House Speaker Dennis Hastert, who currently works as a lobbyist for private corporations and foreign governments.

• More than $326 million in pork will go to the 1.3 million citizens of Hawaii—a per capita rate of $251.78. On the other hand, the 544,270 fine people of Wyoming will receive only $12.28 per person. Take a guess which state has a senator who is chairman of the Senate Appropriations Committee and which state has nary a member on the committee.

• The refusal of many federal employees to fly coach costs taxpayers $146 million annually in flight upgrades.

• The state of Washington sent $1 food-stamp checks to 250,000 households in order to raise state caseload figures and trigger $43 million in additional federal funds.

• Lawmakers diverted $13 million from Hurricane Katrina relief spending to build a museum celebrating the Army Corps of Engineers—the agency partially responsible for the failed levees that flooded New Orleans.

• The Defense Department wasted $100 million on unused airline tickets and never bothered to collect refunds even though the tickets were refundable.

Uncollected refunds? A Grateful Dead archive? One dollar food stamps? It's frustrating, but earmarks and wasteful spending by agencies account for only part of the problem of reckless spending generally. Congress rarely meets a program it doesn't support.

Consider, for example, a bill signed into law in April 2009 called the Serve America Act. This new law will cause more than $5 billion to be spent over the next five years, and in doing so, will begin to remake charity in America and place yet another quintessential American institution under the purview of the government. The law will steer volunteers away from their own choices of volunteer opportunities and toward the choices of bureaucrats.

There are hundreds, perhaps thousands, of examples like this every year, often coated in ostensible good. Early in 2010, a reauthorization bill (take a guess how many times things are *not* reauthorized in Washington . . .) was passed out of the Senate Judiciary Committee to give more than $425 million to the Boys and Girls Clubs of America over the next five years. I have enormous respect for the Boys and Girls Clubs — it is an outstanding organization that has helped countless children across America. And we have provided some state resources in support of certain of its programs. But on what basis are we giving $425 million in federal money on top of more than $600 million given over the past ten years when the club spent more than $2 million on lobbyists and raised over $650 million in private resources the previous year?[31]

This culture of reckless spending is exemplified by another legacy of the New Deal. Agriculture spending, or farm subsidies, is designed to continue the longstanding tradition of farming in America that so many of us cherish. Farming was my life, and I believe our nation is stronger because of the American farmer. But the constant stream of subsidies coming out of Washington, again with good intentions, seriously undermines the small farmer while costing taxpayers billions of dollars.

During a recession in the 1890s, which brought 18 percent unemployment, secretary of agriculture J. Sterling Morton refused to subsidize farming, choosing instead to trim his department's budget by nearly 20 percent and downsize its bureaucracy. He rejected a plea for help from beet-sugar producers, saying, "Those who raise corn should not be taxed to encourage those who desire to raise beets. The power to tax was never vested in a Government for the purpose of building up one class at the expense of other classes."[32]

One hundred years later, between 1995 and 2009, the federal government distributed over $245 billion in farm subsidies.[33] What is astounding is that this year, over half of all farm subsidies are going to commercial farms, which report average household incomes of $200,000.[34] Sometimes the subsidies make absolutely no sense, such as subsidies that go to suburban families for the grass in their backyards.[35] Seriously. Worse yet, this kind of intervention puts Washington bureaucrats smack in the middle of the business of farming. As President Dwight Eisenhower once said, "Farming looks mighty easy when your plow is a pencil and you are a thousand miles from the cornfield."

One of the most egregious results of this kind of interventionist, unconstitutional policy is today's dairy industry. Agriculture Department bureaucrats set the price of milk, and nobody is allowed to offer a lower price.[36] Consider the example of Dutch immigrant Hein Hettinga, who set up a dairy business outside of the federal government controls in the 1990s. He sold milk to grocery stores for 20 cents less than the government-mandated prices and naturally had a booming business. When the dairy interests caught wind of Hettinga's activities, a lobbying blitz ensued, and Congress passed a law in 2006 that crushed his business.[37] He's been tied up in litigation against Washington ever since, fighting for his right to earn a living by providing consumers with affordable milk.

Hettinga was quoted as saying he "had an awakening...it's not totally free enterprise in the United States."[38] The indefensible price controls enforced by running entrepreneurs like Mr. Hettinga out of business mean that Americans pay 26 percent more for milk than they would otherwise.[39] Butter costs twice what it should, and cheese prices are inflated by 50 percent.[40] In effect, Americans are double-taxed by these left-over New Deal farm policies: we pay higher prices in the store for food, while we pay billions of dollars in taxes to fund the Farm Bill, which also happens to be loaded with pork and welfare.

The politics of the Farm Bill illustrate the problem with Washington. As long as your representative gets a goody in the legislation at issue, he has incentive to vote for it. The result, of course, is that the federal grab bag keeps expanding. Congress actually tried to institute market reforms into agricultural policy with the 1996 bill, but this was short lived; later supplemental bills reversed the reforms, and subsidies that were slated to cost $47 billion over the period covered by the 1996 policy ended up with a price tag of $121 billion. The next Farm Bill, in 2002, expanded farm policy even further, adding more crops to be subsidized and even a new "countercyclical" program and a sugar-to-ethanol program.[41]

While President Bush vetoed the 2008 Farm Bill, Congress overrode the veto, passing a bill that propped up even more subsidy programs, created a new "permanent" disaster fund, and created the Average Crop Revenue Election program.[42] The 2008 law was estimated to cost $284 billion through 2012, not counting discretionary programs included in the bill for which Congress must still appropriate funds. We'll see where it really ends up.

But if Congress would just allow the market to work, American consumers would undoubtedly be much better off. New Zealand provides an example. The country faced a financial crisis in the early 1980s and was forced to scale back its government. They began by deregulating the farming industry and removed agricultural subsidies. It has been a fantastic success. New Zealand's farmers are now more productive and more efficient in their land use, and the agricultural sector has become an even stronger part of the country's overall economy.[43] But instead of letting American farmers put their ingenuity to work in the market, Washington perpetuates an illogical program that began as a temporary measure in the New Deal.

The story of centralizing power in Washington always features the same plot, any way you tell it. Wasteful, reckless spending piles debt on top of debt, combined with interventionist policies that interfere with markets and local control. Such spending shows little sign of slowing down, even in the face of crisis. But perhaps even more frightening is the fact that in the midst of this mess, Washington is passing additional legislation that is dramatically transforming the American economy.

Turning the American Economy Upside Down

We are in the midst of an unprecedented assault on free markets. At a time when we need to free up our economy to grow us out of recession and accumulating debt, the government is preventing wealth and job creation through burdensome taxation and regulation — the only effect of which is to stifle economic growth and heighten fiscal crisis. And worse, it is impossible to pick up a newspaper without seeing yet another bailout, "stimulus" plan, or scheme to increase Washington's control over the economy.

We have excise taxes, personal income taxes, corporate income taxes, capital gains taxes, death taxes, Social Security taxes, Medicare taxes, Medicaid taxes, communications fees, and too many other fees to keep up with. How on earth can we possibly compete with all that hanging around our necks? Corporate income taxes in the United States of over 39 percent, for example, rank second in the industrialized world, just behind Japan and well above the average of about 26 percent.[44]

It isn't only a problem of dollars. It's also, and arguably more importantly, a problem of destroying the way in which America works. We are seeing today the culmination of the statist's dream — the literal upending of a unique American way of doing things that has been defined by self-reliance, hard work, faith, a belief in private charity not government, and, perhaps most of all, a devotion to free markets. Consider:

- A $151 billion "stimulus" package offered by the Bush administration in the form of rebate checks in February 2008, in the early stages of a lagging economy, ignoring the need for long-term growth policies in favor of a quick (non) fix.

- In July 2008, the Housing and Economic Recovery Act of 2008, in which the federal government increased loan limits, insured $300 billion in subprime loans, and gave away money in the form of housing tax credits.

- In September 2008, Fannie Mae and Freddie Mac were effectively nationalized to the tune of $100 billion, which has since been raised twice—once in February 2009 to $200 billion, and again in December 2009 to an *unlimited* amount.

- Among many nefarious activities by the federal government, in September 2008, it figuratively put a gun to the head of Bank of America and forced it to buy Merrill Lynch without regard to its fiduciary duty to shareholders.

- In October 2008, the Troubled Asset Relief Program was signed into law, dramatically altering the relationship of government and the markets. It effectively authorized an additional $700 billion in bailout authority over and above the Fannie and Freddie funding, allowing the U.S. Treasury to invest in "troubled assets."

- In 2009, the federal government took over Chrysler and General Motors. In the process, the government decided who would run them and what dealerships would get shut down, and invested billions of dollars in them.

- The federal government directed hundreds of billions of dollars to bail out insurance giant AIG even as the company threw lavish corporate retreats.

- In February 2009, President Obama embarked on the largest single government spending binge known to mankind on signing a stimulus bill of $787 billion.

- In March 2010, Obamacare was signed into law, unconstitutionally forcing an individual mandate on the American people to buy insurance, and in so doing, taking the first steps toward single-payer, government-run health care.
- In 2010, the federal government began efforts to take over the financial markets, because it believes that somehow greater government regulation and political lending standards will prevent another financial crisis like the one that was created by... government regulation and political lending standards. Tellingly, the bill's chief architect, senator Chris Dodd said, "This is about as important as it gets, because it deals with every single aspect of our lives."[45]

Under the misguided and overused notion that there are certain companies that are "too big to fail," these programs turn America upside down, totally undermining the idea of limited government, free markets, and federalism. In the process, they raise the question of whether our government is too big to fix.

Now, I realize there are few if any clean hands among modern politicians, particularly in Washington, on these issues. Indeed, this big-government binge began under the administration of George W. Bush. But, for those who believe there is no distinction between the Republican and Democrat Parties, consider the current state of things. Even though I disagreed with President Bush on certain policies, he took interventionist steps reluctantly and with a vision that they should be temporary. He famously said in a moment that caused many of us to cringe, "I've abandoned free-market principles to save the free-market system." But what he intended to do on a temporary basis, the current regime is pursuing as permanent policy.

For a statist like President Obama, a door cracked for the federal government to solve a national crisis is an open door for pursuing his agenda, behind which is creeping socialism. He sees this as a crisis that must not go to waste. Demonstrating an FDR-like mentality, he said in a speech in April 2009, "We have been called to govern in extraordinary times." Rahm Emanuel made it even more explicit when he compared the current climate to that of the Great Depression, saying, "Every time in a period of crisis...people have reinterpreted what the government can and should do. We're in that moment of time now.... We're defining it as we go. At one level, I'm not sure they knew what the New Deal was when they were doing it."[46]

Now, making the New Deal look like child's play, the Obama administration has gone on a spending spree that would make John Maynard Keynes blush — marked primarily by that so-called stimulus bill of $787 billion. Keep in mind that in current dollars this is an almost-identical amount to the $50 billion in spending of the New Deal... for the *entire period of 1933 to 1940*.[47] One time, one shot — basically the entire (failed) New Deal passed in one big stimulus bill. Now, Obama's budget calls for trillion-dollar deficits every year for the next decade. This would double the debt, as a percentage of GDP, by 2020.[48] When you throw a realistic look at Obamacare into the mix, the picture is even worse.

In the end, some of the programs of the past several years may work. Loans may get repaid. Some companies may be saved. But that can't be the measure of success. The damage caused by this is long term and of the sort that fundamentally undermines freedom and our competitiveness as a nation. This is not the easiest thing to measure, of course, but the *Wall Street Journal* and the Heritage Foundation annually produce the Index of Economic Freedom, which ranks all nations accordingly. This year, the United States dropped to the "mostly free" category for the first time since the ranking began and in so doing fell to eighth place overall, behind Canada and just ahead of Denmark. Admittedly, that is just one ranking, but based on your observations and the above litany of government interventions, do you doubt that America is becoming less economically free?

Is this the way to lead the world in the twenty-first century? We are the nation of Vanderbilt, Carnegie, Morgan, Edison, Ford, Forbes, Gates, Jobs, Dell, and countless others whose names you don't know, like José Cuevas, Jim Eustace, Margaret Martin, Charlie Guluzian, who have started small businesses employing millions of Americans, and all for their piece of the American Dream. We have a front-row seat to the greatest experiment in the history of mankind — a living testament to how much man can achieve when free to benefit from the use of his labor and capital — yet we continue to allow the power brokers in Washington to forsake the principles that built our nation as they are en route to bankrupting it, all while broadening government control over the most intimate parts of our daily lives.

5

No *American Left Alone:*
Health Care, Education,
the Environment, and the
Tyranny of the Modern
Administrative State

A government bureau is the nearest thing to eternal
life we'll ever see on this earth.
— RONALD REAGAN, "A TIME FOR CHOOSING"
SPEECH, 1964[1]

VIRTUALLY EVERY ASPECT OF our lives is managed in some form or fashion by someone in Washington. The federal administrative state has become so far-reaching — having departments or agencies focused on energy, the environment, health care, food, drugs, guns, labor, education, and more — that it is almost impossible to know where it ends. It gets its initial empowerment from Congress, which passes broadly worded statutes, but the unelected employees of these executive agencies are left with the real rule-making authority. These are the "experts" who will decide precisely how your life is affected by federal laws.

Remember when Nancy Pelosi famously said we'll have to pass

Obamacare to "find out what's in it"? Well, that's partly because there was no way for her or any member of Congress or any ordinary citizen to understand the over-2,000-page legislative monstrosity. But it's also because we literally won't know what Obamacare will look like until the regulators over at the Department of Health and Human Services and the IRS — whose ranks will swell by the thousands — write the details of your new health care plan. Ever heard of Nancy-Ann DeParle? She's the director of the White House Office of Health Reform, and she met twice a week with "several dozen top officials to weigh in on the myriad sensitive decisions required to translate the law's mandates into fine print covering one-sixth of the economy."[2]

That is the nature of an administrative state that grows exponentially year-by-year and in which no American is left alone.

The Administrative State — Central to the Progressive Expansion

It goes without saying that the Founding Fathers did not have an administrative state in mind. The Constitution established a limited government of enumerated powers. But, importantly, those powers were separated among three coequal branches — legislative, executive, and judicial. This separation of powers would allow for checks and balances whereby each branch of the government could guard its territory and police the other two. In *Federalist 47,* James Madison discusses the importance of the separation of powers, writing, "The accumulation of all powers, legislative, executive, and judiciary, in the same hands, whether of one, a few, or many ... may justly be pronounced the very definition of tyranny."[3]

The Progressives of the early twentieth century recognized that the Founders' carefully crafted division of authority stood smack-dab in the way of their agenda. Before he became president, Woodrow Wilson was one of those Progressives in academia who called for a new method of government that would better suit his interventionist ambitions. Directly challenging the separation-of-powers model, he wrote that "no living thing can have its organs offset against each other, as checks, and live."[4] It was ideas like this that helped give rise to the behemoth administrative state that exploded during the New Deal.

Some New Dealers admitted it. James Landis served in several important capacities during the New Deal. A dean of the Harvard Law School, he has been called the "single most important intellectual figure in the New Deal" and the "architect of the modern administrative state."[5] Landis provided a peek into the mind-set of Roosevelt's government architects when he wrote, "The insistence upon the compartmentalization of power along triadic lines gave way in the nineteenth century to the exigencies of governance. Without too much political theory but with a keen sense of the practicalities of the situation, agencies were created whose functions embraced the three aspects of government."[6] It is telling that, in Landis's view, the Constitution so carefully crafted by the Founders and ratified by the American citizenry is easily and flippantly dismissed as a nebulous "insistence" that "gave way" to the "exigencies" of government.

The result is almost mind-numbing. Today our federal government includes some fifteen Cabinet-level departments, up from three at the time of our nation's founding. Below those massive departments are some 180 independent agencies, and scores more within the legislative and judicial branches.[7] There are over 2 million employees in today's administrative state (the population of the entire state of New Mexico), 97 percent of whom work in the executive branch. But while some statists like to hide behind the notion that this number has not grown significantly in the past several decades, that's not the full story. The true size of the federal government's employment is millions more — indeed, over 14.6 million even as far back as 2006 — when we account for contractors and others not technically "employed" by the federal government but doing its bidding all the while.[8] All of this personnel deals with the more than 163,000 pages of federal code that requires interpretation, analysis, and application, as well as enforcing and complying with over 4,500 federal laws[9] and 3.7 million words of tax code that even the IRS had to admit "has grown so long that it has become challenging even to figure out how long it is."[10]

But I am not yet finished. Some like to say our governments are appropriately balanced, since there are almost 16.6 million state and local employees[11] (8 million if we exclude schools and hospitals).[12] But, when you consider that these employees are spread across 50 state governments and 87,500 local governments,[13] the number doesn't seem as large — and the federal government controls many of these folks through federal funding and the strings attached to it. In addition to the millions of teachers increasingly funded with federal dollars, for example, about one-third of the funding for Texas Health and Human Services also goes through Washington.

It is by way of this administrative state that the federal government has slowly taken over every aspect of our lives, and it is especially apparent in its involvement in health care.

The Federal State of Health Care

No issue is more critical for the defense of freedom and the American way of life than the preservation of our free-market health care system and the total repeal and dismantling of so-called

Obamacare. President Obama and the Democrats in Congress have thrust upon us a health care scheme that will make any current bureaucracy seem trivial and will destroy our nation's health care system in the process. It is an example of everything that is wrong with the modern administrative state, only on steroids.

This is not hyperbole, for our ability as Americans to have access to the best health care in the world—and our right to make our own personal health care decisions—literally hangs in the balance, as this administration and Democrats on the Hill consolidate power and insert the long tentacles of Washington into every hospital and doctor's office in America. Because the premise of Obamacare is that our health is not our responsibility but the public's.

At its core, Obamacare represents the closest this country has ever come to outright socialism. Those on the Left note that they are unhappy this bill did not go even further— to what they innocuously call a single-payer system, in which government takes over the entire field of medicine. It's not as if they're hiding their intent. President Obama told the AFL-CIO in 2003 while campaigning for the Senate, "I happen to be a proponent of a single-payer health care program," and then added, "We may not get there immediately."[14] Instead of keeping the public option in the bill (thus stirring up the ire of millions of Americans), Democrats instead offered a public plan that competes with private insurance— only the government sets the rules of the competition. The result will be the bankrupting of private plans, and then a public option to rescue health care from the abyss and the supposedly greedy profiteers of private insurance. The liberals are not stupid about health care—they are insidious.

First and foremost, Obamacare mandates that the American people must go out and buy government-approved health insurance in the private market. I defy anyone to show me the clause in the Constitution that gives Washington the authority to do this. It is a total outrage that the federal government would tell an American citizen that he must buy anything from anyone but especially something that concerns his health and the health of his family.

Its problems go well beyond this unconstitutional mandate, however. While that in itself is galling, the other problems are perhaps even more pernicious. The law raises our taxes, empowers the IRS to enforce the plan's provisions, funds abortion,[15] and widely expands the administrative state and federal deficit spending. Senator Jim DeMint (R-SC) called Obamacare "a bureaucratic nightmare...a byzantine network of 159 new federal programs and bureaucracies to make decisions that should be between just the patient and their doctor."[16] He is right.

The issues involved in health care are complex, but the simple explanation of the problem with Obamacare is that federal bureaucrats will be empowered to ration care and make important decisions about our health—even in matters of life and death. Two new bureaucracies have been established—the Patient-Centered Outcomes Research Institute and the Independent Payment Advisory Board—which will soon have the final word on what constitutes "good" medicine. The importance or power of this board is hardly being hidden by the Obama administration. Peter Orszag, the President's former budget director, openly discussed, in a speech to the Economic Club of Washington in April 2010, the "power" of the Independent Payment Advisory Board to reduce costs—which means to ration health care—outside the purview of Congress, and even praised the "inertia" that has now been created in favor of these bureaucrats instead of elected officials.[17] Indeed, Democrats in Congress know how important the board is, having hidden a rule requiring a two-third vote to repeal the board in the 2,000-plus-page legislation.[18]

The net result of this will be government bureaucrats—not your doctor—deciding what the right treatment is for you. Essentially, by attaching different reimbursements (using the current Medicare and Medicaid reimbursement systems) to different procedures, the federal government will be able to induce your doctor to give you the tests and treatments it decides are most cost effective. The scheme is filled with "councils of experts" and panels of various sorts, including a panel that will be empowered to make decisions in matters of life and death in order to contain costs.

Now, my friend Sarah Palin took a lot of heat for calling this as she saw it—the empowerment of death panels. But is she wrong? Sure, there isn't a section titled "death panels" in the law, but that's not how the statist works. The scheme is built around the central premise that federal bureaucrats get to decide a lot of things for you, and they are motivated by controlling costs, redistribution, and "fairness." As one expert, Dr. Alan Garber of Stanford University said, "Being able to say no is the heart of the issue."[19] We give those bureaucrats the power, and they *want* to say no in order to make the system work.

Matters of life and death, indeed. I honestly have no words to describe how frightening this whole scheme is and how badly it undermines freedom. Indeed, as Daniel Hannan, a British member of Parliament who knows socialized medicine firsthand, said, "The idea that this, of all countries, could put into the power of a state bureaucracy decisions over what kind of medical treatment you get, literally whether you can live or die, is deeply un-American."[20]

Most concerning is Obama's appointment of Dr. Donald Berwick to head up the Centers for Medicare and Medicaid Services (CMS). The President was savvy enough to appoint this Massachusetts doctor in a recess appointment rather than the typical Senate confirmation process, knowing that a Senate hearing would likely spark public outrage and possibly derail Berwick's confirmation. Berwick is an outspoken fan both of health care rationing and the British health care system, which is a model of socialized medicine. Berwick once said, "The decision is not whether or not we will ration care—the decision is whether we will ration with our eyes open."[21] He has also opined that the government "can make a sensible social decision" and deny access to certain medical care because it is "so expensive that our taxpayers have better use for those funds."[22] Shouldn't *your* doctor make that decision? Remember those "death panels"?

Berwick's economic philosophy about health care is no less blatant: "Any health care funding plan that is just, equitable, civilized, and humane must, must redistribute wealth from the richer among us to the poorer and the less fortunate. Excellent health care is by definition redistributional."[23] Unfortunately, it seems the more government intervenes, the smaller the supply of medicine there is to go around. If the proposed Medicare cuts are taken as expected, the chief actuary at CMS predicts that as many as 15 percent of hospitals may close.[24] In what world is a health care system that provides *less* care a better one?

Obamacare only makes matters worse for the existing broken systems of Medicare, Medicaid, and CHIP. Seniors are expected to see major Medicare cuts, particularly in Medicare Advantage. Medicare has largely crowded out the market for private health insurance for seniors, and it has done so in a way that has driven up costs that must be paid by future generations. It is estimated that to pay for the future funding gaps in Medicare, Congress would have to put $80 trillion into an interest-bearing account today (when the U.S. GDP is only in the $15 trillion range).[25] Once again, the federal government spends money it doesn't have on programs that states, individuals, or private companies could likely do cheaper and better.

The situation looks even bleaker for Medicaid recipients. The primary problem with Medicaid right now is that there are too many beneficiaries and not enough doctors or funding. Obamacare worsens both the supply and the demand. To achieve the goal of universal coverage (in fact, some 23 million Americans will still be uninsured by 2019),[26] Obamacare simply makes more people eligible for Medicaid. As if the system were not already strained enough, this expansion will prompt an especially huge surge in spending because those newly eligible for coverage will largely represent high-risk groups that will demand more expensive care.

Moreover, with even fewer doctors available because of the spending cuts, waiting times and the costs to see primary care physicians will skyrocket. One national survey found that 45 percent of physicians might think about quitting as a result of this legislation (that is, not just stop refusing Medicaid patients but quitting the field entirely).[27] Obamacare will cause Medicaid costs in Texas alone to rise $4.5 billion between 2014 and 2019,[28] leaving Texans the hardest hit by unfunded Medicaid liability as a percentage of our state's General Funds.[29]

Massachusetts provides a great example of laboratories of democracy in action. Massachusetts enacted universal health care on a statewide basis in 2006, including an individual mandate and an expansion of the Medicaid rolls. Since then, the waiting times to see a doctor in Massachusetts have nearly doubled,[30] and the costs are so out of control that a special commission has already recommended that the state insurance plans "limit coverage to services that produce the highest value when considering both clinical effectiveness and cost"[31] — that is, rationing care based on the government's perceived cost-benefit calculation. Is it any surprise that this is the state from which Dr. Berwick hails?

In addition to the fact that Obamacare does not cure the ills it claims to, this legislation also represents a *huge* increase in the size of the federal government and its ever-growing spending. Experts suggest that Obamacare will cost $2.7 trillion over its first 10 years and will add more than $352 billion to the national debt.[32] Sixteen thousand five hundred additional people are expected to be hired by the IRS to enforce these measures, at a cost of $669 billion.[33] We can expect that to come in the form of payroll tax hikes, taxes on so-called Cadillac insurance plans (which will soon be most of them, based on the accounting method), new investment taxes, sales taxes on pharmaceuticals and medical devices, and on and on.

Finally, Obamacare represents a huge blow to businesses, both big and small, and thus to jobs. The Congressional Budget Office estimates that the penalties associated with the employer mandate in Obamacare will cost businesses $52 billion between 2014 and 2019.[34] And some of that effect is immediate: AT&T announced that it was taking a $1 billion charge in the first quarter of 2010 to satisfy the requirements of another bureaucracy, the U.S. Securities and Exchange Commission, that corporations restate their earnings to reflect the present value of their long-term health liabilities. Verizon wrote down $970 million, and other large, productive companies that employ thousands of Americans similarly had to set aside huge portions of their future expected earnings — earnings that could be used to invest in innovations or to pay the salaries of employees — to offset the costs they will face from Obamacare mandates.

It's also worth noting that it might actually be cheaper for many companies to simply pay the penalty rather than to comply with the employer mandate, turning Obama's promise that most Americans will be able to keep their insurance into a lie. If companies opt for the penalty, their employees will have to go elsewhere for their (mandated) coverage. Even if companies still choose to offer health insurance, though, the Department of Health and Human Services — part of Obama's own administration — has estimated in an internal memo that more than two-thirds of companies (and more like 80 percent of small businesses) will have to change their current insurance plans under Obamacare.[35] Given that most private health insurance today is administered through one's employer, a lot of people will not be allowed to keep their current health insurance.

Among other provisions of Obamacare that will cause headaches and wallet aches for businesses—and the economy—are new reporting requirements for 1099 tax forms, which will significantly increase the administrative burden of running a business, particularly a small one. If you do more than $600 of business with Office Depot, for instance, you will have to send them a 1099. Should you send that to their headquarters or to the local store where you purchased chairs and copy paper? It's an administrative nightmare. Additionally, the provision requiring calorie counts on all chain-restaurant menus will cost those companies as much as $2,000 per store,[36] and posting calorie counts on vending machines will cost those businesses over $56 million dollars for the first year.[37] Taken together, all of these new laws will make it harder and more expensive for businesses to operate and to employ people at a time when productivity and jobs are what America needs most.

Given the federal government's mind-boggling overreach in requiring each citizen to buy health insurance, what is next? It sounds silly to think about the possibility of the federal government requiring you to buy, say, air filters for your house, or a certain kind of toothbrush, or certain kinds of food, but if it makes you healthier, what's to stop them? There is no end to this road once we start down it.

Health care is a tricky subject in America because it is so critical to every one of us on a personal level. No one wants any American to go without the health care he or she needs. But that's not what this debate is all about. It's about control. And as bad as the situation with Medicare and Medicaid is, Obamacare represents an enormous and dangerous step closer to the socialist abyss.

Federal Intervention in Education

Education is another of those areas of our lives that had remained primarily a local and state affair until federal intervention during the Great Society. In 1965, LBJ signed the Elementary and Secondary Education Act, which for the first time introduced federal dollars into local public schools and, consequently, federal influence into how we at the local level were choosing to educate our children. By 1994, there were already 13,400 federally funded employees in state education agencies working to implement these federal initiatives at the local level. And while the federal government was providing only 7 percent of overall education funding, it was causing 41 percent of the state administrative burden.[38]

This federal intrusion got markedly worse in 2001, with the reauthorization of the ESEA in the form of No Child Left Behind (NCLB). Sometimes referred to as the cornerstone of President Bush's administration, the bill was shepherded through Congress by Senator Ted Kennedy (D-MA) and represented the bipartisan doubling down of federal involvement in the education of our children. The law requires states to follow a host of very specific federal requirements to conduct standardized tests, to put in place measures of performance, and to then take "corrective action" if the standards are not met. Technically, NCLB does not force states to comply with these federal standards. Rather, just like the spending hook used to induce compliance for seat-belt and drinking-age laws, the federal government reaches into our pockets, takes out wads of tax dollars, and then says that we can have them back only if we comply with federal instructions. Sure, we can opt out—but if we do, the federal government will just take the money we've put into the pot and distribute it to other states. And the Supreme Court says that's not coercive...

Though compliance with NCLB did mean that states received

back some of the money they put into the pot, compliance itself was not free. The state of Connecticut, for example, estimated that their compliance costs for NCLB in 2007 alone were more than $17 million;[39] for Virginia, the number was closer to $20 million per year.[40]

Do you think there would have been significant Republican opposition? Nope. In the House, Republicans voted 185–34 in favor of NCLB, while in the Senate the vote among Republicans was 43–6.[41] Unfortunately, this willingness to turn power over to Washington was driven in significant part by the desire to further expand federal faith-based initiatives and to provide for the increased possibility of school choice. This is a perfect example of Republicans losing sight of the fact that perfectly laudable policy choices at the local level are not appropriate (much less constitutional) at the federal level. This is not consistent with a belief in a limited federal government of enumerated powers. Worse, the Department of Education is now unfettered in its ability to interfere in the affairs of local government and employs 4,200 people, with an annual budget of close to $47 billion (excluding student loans) plus billions more in stimulus dollars.[42]

The transition to the Obama administration has only made things worse, of course. For instance, provisions of the No Child Left Behind Act that I agree with include some limits to the role of the federal government in education. Specifically, NCLB restricts the federal government from enacting national curriculum standards, creating a national testing system, and establishing a national database with information about every student.[43] That law is still on the books and has not been changed by Congress. However, now the Department of Education is enacting the very things prohibited by NCLB by claiming it is doing so under the authority of the massive American Recovery and Reinvestment Act (stimulus bill).

The federal government's interference in the state education system in Texas reached a crescendo this year when the President introduced $4.3 billion in Race to the Top funding. As a precondition of eligibility just to compete for the funding, the President required that states endorse the Common Core State Standards Initiative, a "voluntary" effort by the states to establish national curriculum standards. I have said it before, and I will say it again: The academic standards of Texas are not for sale. We will retain our sovereign authority to decide how to educate our children.

While it's an abomination that the federal government takes so much of our money in the first place, it's unconscionable that it gives it back to us only on the condition that we spend it in the manner the federal government wishes. It's interesting to note, too, that while a number of Texas's school superintendents shortsightedly support this federal overreach, even they recognized a common problem when the federal government gets involved in education: the money goes to teachers' unions, not to the students it purports to benefit. As Houston school superintendent Terry Grier complained, the teachers on the ground here in Texas wanted to use the ill-gotten funds to "help close the achievement gap" and for "reform initiatives."[44] Legislators and bureaucrats in Washington, however, demanded that the money be used *only* to create additional layers of staff, just what the unions would want.

Only Washington Cares About the Environment

Even if you live outside Texas, you have probably seen headlines regarding our lawsuits against the Environmental Protection Agency. Our dispute with the EPA in particular illustrates how Washington's command-and-control environmental bureaucracy is destroying federalism and individuals' ability to make their own economic decisions. It also proves that, like all bureaucracies from the dawn of society, the environment the EPA is most concerned about protecting is its own turf.

In May 2010, Al Armendariz, the regional EPA director whose territory includes Texas, announced that he was invalidating the operating permit required under the federal Clean Air Act (CAA) for a refinery in Corpus Christi, Texas.[45] The CAA, which has been law since 1970, establishes federal pollution-control standards but delegates to states the authority to issue and oversee the permits required by the law.

The EPA under President Obama doesn't care much for Texas's innovative flexible-permitting system, which establishes pollution caps for entire facilities rather than for each source (like a smoke-stack) within the facility. This flexible approach requires refineries and other businesses to contain their overall emissions, therefore satisfying the federal standards, but allows them the leeway to determine how best and most efficiently to do so. It was put in place under Democratic governor Ann Richards while Bill Clinton was president, and was never disapproved by the federal bureaucrats. In June 2010, the EPA broadened its takeover, invalidating all 122 flexible permits issued by the Texas Commission on Environmental Quality (TCEQ) and dictating that these facilities apply directly to the EPA for new permits.[46]

The EPA must have stepped in to stop a major pollution problem, right? Actually, Texas's commonsense system has been hugely successful in tackling air pollution. Over the past decade, Texas has achieved a 22 percent reduction in ozone and a 46 percent reduction in nitrogen oxide (NOx) emissions, outpacing the rest of the country, which achieved only a 27 percent reduction in NOx.[47] Texas electricity generators have the eleventh lowest NOx rates among all states, and Houston is second only to Atlanta in the total percent decrease in ozone for metropolitan areas since 2000, this while Houston's population increased by 20 percent.[48]

Not a single Texas county is in nonattainment for fine particulate matter (PM 2.5), one of the pollutants with the greatest effect on human health.[49] Another part of the Texas success story: although the CAA allows them, there are no grandfathered facilities in the state. Our flexible-permitting program was designed to entice these older, dirtier facilities to clean themselves up even though they were not required to under federal law.[50]

Texas has made great strides in fighting air pollution while absorbing millions more people and supporting the most dynamic economy in the country. It isn't necessary to bludgeon job creators with hefty fines and penalties in order to make progress; it is better to work with business and harness American innovation—the same innovation that drives our economic success—in the realm of pollution control. Texans living in the communities affected by pollution have a real incentive to keep the environment clean. We want to enjoy clean lakes, rivers, and beaches, and clean air when we jog in the neighborhood. Texas already had established water- and air-pollution programs before Congress inserted itself with the CAA and the Clean Water Act. We also work here, and we have figured out how to protect the environment while fostering business and creating jobs.[51]

Given Texas's record of successfully reducing air pollution, it is clear the EPA's takeover is about only one thing: control. Mr. Armendariz could not say that Texas's air would be cleaner today if his preferred system had been in place.[52] What he did say is that he's confused by the flexible-permitting system and that it's too hard for his army of bureaucrats to police.[53] The EPA might not have the initiative to understand it, but as Mark R. Vickery, the executive director of the TCEQ, has said, "The proof is in the pudding. The air has gotten tremendously cleaner."[54] Texas's fight to preserve a commonsense *and successful* air-quality program is a small window into how the federal environmental bureaucracy has intruded into our lives, and it should focus your attention on what these people are doing to our liberties in the name of a one-size-fits-all regulatory regime.

Despite overwhelming majorities of Democrats in Congress, environmental statists could not (yet, thankfully) shove their climate security bill designed to cut emissions of greenhouse gases—dubbed cap and trade—through this past session. Moderate Democrats recognized the economic devastation that would visit their states if they slapped a de facto energy tax on the entire economy.[55] The statists are now asking the administrative state to do through regulatory fiat what they could not persuade enough elected legislators to do through the constitutionally appropriate lawmaking process. It appears that the Clean Air Act will be the vehicle used to regulate carbon emissions. Applied to carbon—which it was never intended to cover—the economic effects could be absolutely devastating.

That is because under the CAA, any facility that emits a certain level of regulated substance—here greenhouse gases—would be required to jump through all the federally mandated permitting hoops in order to build or modify any buildings.[56] By the EPA's own estimates, this could affect 6 *million* sources of carbon emissions, including 1,354,760 commercial buildings.[57] These types of applications are a destructive burden for those caught in the federal snare, imposing significant costs in time and treasure.[58] The Heritage Foundation estimates that regulation of carbon emissions by the EPA would prevent $7 trillion in economic activity and cost 3 million manufacturing jobs by 2029.[59]

The impacts of such an unprecedented regulatory overreach are even scaring significant numbers of Democrats, who are trying to stop the EPA from regulating carbon for at least two years so that the next Congress can have a crack at passing a climate bill that will be less destructive than the EPA's sledgehammer regulation under the CAA.[60] How this plays out, only time will tell. Often, Democrats themselves are the canaries in the coal mine for their party, sending warning signals of trouble to come when their leadership goes too far. For example, they have seen the headlines in the past year about doctored data related to global warming. They know that we have been experiencing a cooling trend, that the complexities of the global atmosphere have often eluded the most sophisticated scientists, and that draconian policies with dire economic effects based on so-called science may not stand the test of time. Quite frankly, when science gets hijacked by the political Left, we should all be concerned.

Al Gore's ego must have taken a tremendous bruising in the aftermath of the 2000 election, when he was so close to victory he could taste it. As time passed, we began to see the real Al Gore—not the contrived version that ran for president in earth tones, but the liberal extremist who took a hatchet to President Bush in front of the MoveOn.org faithful. Gore found something more satiating to his ego than the presidency. He found a global cause, and he became the prophet who could protect us from Armageddon. Soon he took his PowerPoint presentation around the globe, raising concerns about melting icebergs and undersized polar bears. The Left embraced him like never before. Hollywood toasted him as their hero. The Nobel Committee gave him a peace prize. He won an Oscar. And it's all one contrived phony mess that is falling apart under its own weight. Al Gore is a prophet all right, a false prophet of a secular carbon cult, and now even moderate Democrats aren't buying it.

Financial Intervention

The financial crisis and its "resolution" in the summer of 2010 present another example of the kind of government approach that suggests the only way to solve a problem is to throw more money and bigger government at it. Fundamentally, the financial crisis of 2008 was the product of a number of forces. Significant among them were the federal government's mandate that banks provide a certain number of loans, that Fannie Mae and Freddie Mac existed to purchase those loans (thereby hedging the banks' risk and encouraging banks to make loans that a free market would never sustain), and the Federal Reserve's monetary policy of extremely low interest rates over a long period of time. These government interventions in the free market led to a bubble that eventually burst.

To solve this free-market failure, though, Washington Democrats decided that we needed more government intervention. How much more? A lot, it turns out. The new law is estimated to require at least 243 new formal rule makings by 11 different federal agencies.[61] Counting new rule makings *authorized* by the law, in addition to the minimum of 243 that are *mandated,* the total could actually be 533.[62] The new law has thus been described by the *Wall Street Journal* as "30 times more complicated than Sarbanes-Oxley," the burdens of which, despite only requiring 16 new regulations, have been extremely harmful to the competitiveness of American businesses.[63]

As difficult as it is to contain Washington, it is far easier when the people can at least head to the voting booths to have a say about the laws and the people that govern their lives. When the elected branches of the federal government punt to the undemocratic administrative state, then the states and the people have effectively lost any control over the laws by which they are bound. Worse, the people are left hoping that the bureaucrats will allow them to have input. For example, citing the "significant rulemaking envisioned under the new [financial reform] law," the Securities and

Exchange Commission announced in July that it will go beyond the normal procedures, offering "the public...an opportunity to voice its views before rules or amendments are even proposed as well as to see what others are `saying to the agency about these issues."[64]

The truth is that there is a better way to ensure that local communities are represented in government. If the Constitution were shown the appropriate respect, Washington regulation writers wouldn't have to worry about underrepresented views, because they wouldn't have control over them in the first place. Perhaps more important, we wouldn't have to prostrate ourselves before Washington, praying that they consider our concerns while writing their rules.

6

Nine Unelected Judges Tell Us How to Live

*If the policy of the Government upon vital questions
affecting the whole people is to be irrevocably fixed by
decisions of the Supreme Court ... the people will have
ceased to be their own rulers, having to that extent
practically resigned their Government, into the hands
of that eminent tribunal.*

— ABRAHAM LINCOLN, FIRST INAUGURAL ADDRESS,
MARCH 4, 1861[1]

ON THE MOST DIFFICULT questions of morality and how
we choose to live, the notion that the people govern themselves, be
it individually or through local and state government, is today
mostly fiction. The Supreme Court — filled with nine unelected
and unaccountable judges appointed to the bench for life — long
ago wrested away from the people the power to decide what is
right and what is wrong and, at the most fundamental level, how
we should live our lives. Nothing could be more offensive to the
concept of liberty and the principle of federalism.

Liberty requires that we be able to decide fundamental questions for ourselves or through the democratic process rather than
wait with bated breath every time the Supreme Court meets
for the latest pronouncement on a matter of conscience. And, of

course, this is what our Constitution was designed to ensure. So the Court, above all else, should be steadfast in its commitment to the preservation of liberty and in its responsibility to uphold those fundamental constitutional principles that safeguard a general deference to the people. But it is not.

Instead, as one scholar put it, the justices of the Court act as the "Grand Ayatollahs" of the Constitution and, ultimately then, of the people—able to invalidate their will on a whim.[2] Justice Charles Evans Hughes pointed out in a speech in 1907 (before joining the Supreme Court) that "we are under a Constitution, but the Constitution is what the judges say it is."[3] Hardly the obvious intent of the Founders, regrettably it is the way of things today. To whom may the people realistically appeal when the Court arrogantly chooses to hide behind the Constitution while it implements its own policy choices? No one.

That the Court makes policy can hardly be debated—and that many of these policy choices affect the citizen at the core of his personal conscience is equally beyond question. Consider that it is our courts that routinely decide, with little or no chance of further appeal, how and where we may and may not pray to God, when life begins, whether contraception must be allowed to be sold, whether and how we can celebrate religious holidays, what level of pornography and vulgarity must be allowed, whether those other than man and woman must be allowed to marry, what level of discrimination may or even must be carried out (in the name of ending discrimination), whether a state must allow women to attend an all-male military academy, who may be executed and whether we may execute criminals at all, and generally any issue involving social preferences, morality, and our collective concept of right and wrong.

Should we be surprised? Numerous Founders were skeptical of the power granted the judiciary and predicted that it would quickly trample on any notion of a limited government of separated powers. Jefferson was perhaps the most skeptical of the judiciary, and history has shown this comment from an 1821 letter to be quite prescient: "The germ of dissolution of our Federal Government is in the constitution of the Federal Judiciary — an irresponsible body (for impeachment is scarcely a scare-crow), working like gravity by night and by day, gaining a little today and a little tomorrow, and advancing its noiseless step like a thief...until all shall be usurped from the States, and the government be consolidated into one."[4]

The Court knows no limit to its ability to share its wisdom with the people. But it is the Court's intrusion into personal matters of morality and conscience that is most troubling. Judge Robert Bork, in a book he edited titled *A Country I Do Not Recognize,* summarized well, along with several other legal scholars, how the Court has arrogantly inserted itself into decisions involving the basic values of the American people:

> Traditional values are being jettisoned and self-government steadily whittled away. The American people have no vote on these transformations; efforts by legislatures to set limits to cultural change...are routinely, and almost casually, thwarted.... The complaint here is not that old virtues are eroding and new values rising.... What is objectionable is that...a natural evolution of the moral balance is blocked and a minority morality is forced upon us by judicial decree.... This...was described by Justice Antonin Scalia in a dissent: "What secret knowledge, one must wonder, is breathed into...Justices of this Court, that enables them to discern that a practice which the text of the Constitution does not clearly proscribe, and which our people have regarded as constitutional for 200 years, is in fact

unconstitutional? ... Day by day, case by case, [the Supreme Court] is busy designing a Constitution for a country I do not recognize."[5]

That is the idea in a nutshell, if you ask me — the notion that America is fast becoming "a country I do not recognize." Issue by issue, on matters of the utmost importance to the people, the Court is telling us what to do. Frankly, whether we win or lose the arguments, it's indicative of the Court's power over freedom that we must check every decision we make with the Court. And, to be honest, it hits pretty close to home more times than not.

Since I have been governor, a significant number of cases involving Texas or Texans have gone to the U.S. Supreme Court. From posting the Ten Commandments in the public square to our right to execute a murdering rapist who happens to be a foreign national, we have had to kiss the ring of the Court and have done so, sometimes successfully, sometimes not. Texans have long been involved in significant decisions before the Court, and often we have been told we can't do something. To name a few: *Roe v. Wade* (legalizing abortion), *Plyler v. Doe* (requiring the education of children who are illegal immigrants), *Lawrence v. Texas* (outlawing anti-sodomy laws), *Santa Fe Independent School District v. Doe* (prohibiting student-led prayer at football games), *League of Latin American Citizens v. Perry* (ordering the reconfiguration of a congressional district), and numerous others. It seems Texans have a different view of the world than do the nine oligarchs in robes.

I could write a book on this topic — one chapter doesn't allow nearly enough room. But several specific areas of judicial activism are worth noting, because they give a brief glimpse into the provocative arrogance of the Court and, more important, they strike at the heart of who we are as a people and demonstrate why the

Court's intervention prevents states from being able to govern according to the wishes of the people.

Our Ability to Punish Criminals

Through the police power, states have the right to determine what should or should not be lawful behavior and to administer punishments accordingly. One of the things that the people of Texas have consistently believed is that for our most egregious criminals, the death penalty can be the appropriate punishment. They particularly feel that way about rapists-murderers.

Two cases in particular highlight the extent to which the people are forced to check their view of what should be an appropriate punishment with the Supreme Court. First is the case of *Kennedy v. Louisiana,* which involved a sentence of death for a man convicted of rape.[6] The details of this case are horrifying, but they demonstrate just how out of touch with America the Court truly is.

Patrick Kennedy was sentenced to death not just for rape, but for the rape of his eight-year-old stepdaughter. Her violation was particularly brutal. The little girl suffered massive trauma to her genital area. The injuries were so severe that she required emergency invasive surgery to attempt to repair the damage. The thought of this brutal rape is enough to make one want to place this man in the middle of a Clint Eastwood Western and walk away.

Kennedy refused a plea deal that would have taken the death penalty off the table. He was then convicted under a 1995 Louisiana statute that provided for the death penalty for anyone convicted of raping a child under twelve (it is not hard to believe that our Cajun neighbors and the citizens of five other states agree that such a crime merits the death penalty). A jury of his peers sentenced him to death, and Kennedy immediately appealed to the Louisiana Supreme Court, where he was denied. He then appealed directly to the United States Supreme Court.

Texas supported Louisiana. Our able solicitor general Ted Cruz argued the case on behalf of Texas and eight other states, defending the authority of democratically elected legislatures to determine the appropriate punishment for the very worst rapists.

The Court, in an opinion written by Justice Anthony Kennedy, ruled the law unconstitutional, citing the prohibition in the Eighth Amendment against cruel and unusual punishment. Now, considering that the Supreme Court in 1972 halted the death penalty despite the fact that the Constitution actually includes in its very text a provision for *capital crimes,* only to allow it again a few years later, one might begin to question whether the Constitution had anything at all to do with their reasoning.[7] In his infinite wisdom, Justice Kennedy wrote, "In most cases justice is not better served by terminating the life of the perpetrator rather than confining him and preserving the possibility that he and the system will find ways to allow him to understand the enormity of his offense."[8] Really? What part of that is not making policy?

Then there's a case that brought significant international attention to my state in 2008. In *Medellin v. Texas,* two young high-school girls, Jennifer Ertman (age 14) and Elizabeth Pena (age 16), were brutally raped and murdered by gang members in Houston, Texas.[9] They ran into the gang when returning home from a party, and then were raped for over an hour and strangled to death with shoelaces. One of those gang members was a Mexican national named José Medellin.

Medellin confessed to the crime five days later, and a Texas jury sentenced him to death. He appealed based primarily on his contention that because he had not been notified of his right to contact the Mexican Consulate, Texas was violating the terms of an international treaty, the Vienna Convention on Consular Relations. He lost his first appeal, but after the International Court of Justice (also known as the World Court) ruled that Medellin and 50 other Mexican nationals were entitled to review and reconsideration, he continued forward. Somewhat shockingly, to me at least, President Bush then issued a memorandum attempting to order Texas and other states to review convictions of those not apprised of their consular rights.

The case proceeded to the U.S. Supreme Court, where Solicitor General Cruz again argued our case. Neither I nor my friend Texas attorney general Greg Abbott believed that the United States should be forced to obey the World Court or that the President had the authority to order the state courts to do so. In a 6–3 opinion authored by Chief Justice John Roberts, the Court agreed, and Medellin was executed on August 5, 2008. Amazingly, however, *three* justices did not agree, perhaps believing instead that international law should trump the laws of Texas. They would argue that this was not their reasoning, but is there anything else to conclude?

There are numerous other examples. But, in the end, the states know best how they wish to punish criminals and for what crimes. Are we perfect? No. In Texas, we have been working diligently to advance the use of DNA and to make sure we have as many safeguards as are prudent to ensure the integrity of that system. But our system works very well, and for Washington, and in particular the Supreme Court, to step in and tell us, our friends in Louisiana, or any other state, whether it is right to execute a heinous criminal — or tell us how to carry out justice — is the height of arrogance and disregards federalism at its most basic level.

Our Right to Faith in the Public Square

Is there anything more fundamental to the founding of our nation than the right to the "free exercise of religion" as guaranteed in the First Amendment to the Constitution? Yet, the Supreme Court, focusing almost solely on the Establishment Clause — the intent of which was to prevent a national established church — has so meddled with the very idea that we should be able to worship freely, that the mere mention of God or any exhibition of faith in Him is close to being scrubbed from the public square.

It is for that reason that, led by Attorney General Abbott, we fought to ensure that we could continue to display the Ten Commandments outside the Texas State Capitol Building in Austin.[10] We won the case, *Van Orden v. Perry,* against constitutional challenge in another 5–4 decision. But quite tellingly, on the exact same day, the Court told two county courthouses in Kentucky that they could *not* display the Ten Commandments — all hinging on the musings of Justice Stephen Breyer.[11] Once again, the people are left wondering what set of circumstances might appeal to one justice, on the right day when he's in the right mood, so that they might exercise faith freely.

As is reasonably well known now, the Court turned 175 years of American history on its head when in 1962 it ended state-sponsored school prayer in New York and in 1963 ended the reading of the Lord's Prayer and Bible verses in schools in Pennsylvania.[12] By 1992, the Court had extended these restrictions to moments of silence and to prayer at public graduation ceremonies. You see, public prayer is deemed part of the "establishment" of religion, and thus, both principles of federalism and the right to free exercise of religion are ignored and trampled on. Someone should mention something about the travesty of public prayer to the Congress, whose chaplain leads the Senate and the House in prayer at the opening of every session.

But it wouldn't stop there. My friend U.S. senator John Cornyn, when he was attorney general of Texas, argued the now-famous *Santa Fe Independent School District v. Doe* case against a constitutional challenge to student-led prayer at high-school football games.[13] Unfortunately, in a 6–3 decision (with Chief Justice Rehnquist and Justices Thomas and Scalia in dissent), the Court held that the prayer could not continue in this Texas town despite the fact that the policy had been changed so that students voted to decide whether to have the prayer in the first place. As then Chief Justice Rehnquist noted in his dissent, the opinion "bristle[d] with hostility to all things religious in public life."[14]

The Court itself has created a complex and entirely incomprehensible morass of multipronged tests to determine what is permissible. In the process, the Court has cleansed the schools of prayer, restricted how funds can be used in support of religious groups, prohibited some religious displays, and otherwise set out on a course to diminish or eliminate religious expression in the public square, ignoring the Founders' reservation of such decisions to the states.

The Court has helped develop a culture of litigation against our closely held values, like prayer. In 2004, Senator Cornyn held a hearing on this topic in his capacity as chairman of the Senate Subcommittee on the Constitution, and Texas-based Liberty Institute submitted a document into the public record with 51 pages detailing blatant hostility to religious expression — oftentimes the result of assaults by the American Civil Liberties Union or similar groups.[15] The report details the hostility in stark examples.

A 12-year-old girl in Missouri was reprimanded for praying before lunch; a second-grade girl in Wisconsin was prohibited from passing out Valentines with religious messages; two sisters in Houston, Texas, had their Bibles confiscated and thrown away; and this from New Jersey:

> The ACLU, along with some citizens, filed a lawsuit to challenge a display consisting of a crèche with traditional figures, a lighted tree, urns, candy cane banners, a menorah and signs commenting on celebrating diversity and freedom, as well as wishing passer-bys Merry Christmas and Happy Hanukkah.[16]

While in many cases, the lower courts did the right thing and protected the religious liberty in question, the reality is that this kind of atmosphere is the direct result of the Supreme Court's totally incomprehensible jurisprudence in this area of the law.

Particularly troubling for me has been the assault by the Left, especially the ACLU, on the Boy Scouts of America, an organization near and dear to my heart. I was a Boy Scout and eventually achieved the honor of becoming an Eagle Scout, as did my son, Griffin. In 2008, I wrote a book titled *On My Honor,* in which I give some of the history of the scouts and highlight the perpetual attack on that great organization. Since 1975, the Boy Scouts of America has been drawn into more than 30 lawsuits "attacking its values."[17] The bulk of these cases have dealt with challenges to the organization's membership requirement to believe in God, to be male, and not to be openly homosexual. That is how the organization wishes to assemble. Fortunately, in a challenge by an openly gay man who was prevented from being a scout leader that went to the Supreme Court in 2000, the Boy Scouts' freedom of association as guaranteed by the First Amendment was upheld. But it was yet another 5–4 decision, leaving us to wonder if the values the Boy Scouts cherish will be allowed to continue. Apparently, it will depend on who happens to be on the Court.

There you have the clarity of the Court's position on freedom of religion in America. As a result of activism that makes the Court's jurisprudence on the First Amendment almost incomprehensible, the ability of the people to practice their faith freely is jeopardized. Instead of being able to gather with like-minded individuals town by town and state by state to celebrate our most basic, cherished, and fundamental beliefs, we are left living in a society not of our own making but of the Court's.

Our Right to Keep and Bear Arms

We Texans like our guns. We don't like meddlesome statists who want to infringe on our right to keep and bear them. Fortunately, in this area of the law, we are in better shape than in others, but only barely, and mainly because we have been diligent in fighting legislation in this area in the first place, giving the Court fewer opportunities to be active. There have really been only a handful of seminal cases regarding the Second Amendment compared with the scores of cases affecting most of our other rights.

First, the downside — the Court has allowed Congress to use the Commerce Clause to extend its tentacles into the regulation of firearms in a way that stretches an appropriate understanding of the word "commerce." For example, the Gun Control Act of 1968 (GCA) was passed under the guise of commerce to massively increase federal regulation of firearms. The law greatly restricts private transactions of firearms in a number of ways and prohibits certain classes of individuals from possessing a firearm. For example, under 18 U.S.C. §922(g)(1), it is unlawful for a felon to possess a firearm. Now, I believe that is a reasonable law—after all, Texas has an almost identical law. But is this a federal issue? Well, the federal statute states that the gun must be possessed "in or affecting commerce." And thus, Congress reaches out and touches things it generally was not given the constitutional authority to regulate.

On a more positive note, this stretch of "commerce" hit a wall in 1995 for the first time since the New Deal when the Supreme Court ruled (again, 5–4) that the federal prohibition of guns in school zones was a bridge too far.[18] The impact of the ruling is unclear as a result of subsequent non-gun-related cases I mentioned earlier, but it is notable for sending a signal that there is a limit, however vague, to "interstate commerce." As Justice Thomas wrote in concurrence, "Our case law has drifted far from the original understanding of the Commerce Clause. In a future case, we ought to temper our Commerce Clause jurisprudence in a manner that... is more faithful to the original understanding of that Clause."[19]

In the past several years, there have been two extraordinary moments for gun rights in the United States. In 2008, the Court ruled (again, 5–4) that in federal territories (such as the District of Columbia, in this case) there is an individual right to keep and bear arms, and thus ruled the D.C. law that prohibited possession of a handgun unconstitutional.[20] More important, in *McDonald v. Chicago* earlier this year (in 2010), the Court applied the Second Amendment to the states and ruled (again, 5–4) Chicago's similar prohibition unconstitutional while affirming its earlier holding that it is indeed an individual right and not somehow a collective right of the militia.[21]

Texas took a lead role in both cases. Our state brought together

38 states in defense of the right to keep and bear arms, filing briefs in both cases in support of the Second Amendment.

Now, I know the next question. "But Governor Perry, you say you believe in federalism, but how, then, can you applaud the Court's telling a state it cannot regulate handguns?" The answer is simple. I believe there are fundamental rights, expressed in the Constitution and Bill of Rights. The right to keep and bear arms is one of those fundamental rights. Given that fundamental rights are applied to the states, then so should the Second Amendment be applied to the states. The Commerce Clause should not be used as a catchall for statists to tell the people of Texas or any other state how it should handle the regulation of firearms or any other fundamental right.

Our Ability to Protect Innocent Life

But perhaps no issue and no Supreme Court decision has polarized America more and defined the notion of judicial activism more clearly than the matter of abortion and the judge-made law that caused the dreadful procedure to become commonplace in American society. This issue has come to define much of American political discourse of the years since the *Roe v. Wade* decision in 1973. But the real story is not the politics but the innocent unborn who have been denied the right to life by judicial fiat.

The way this came about is simple. First, the Court decided in 1963 that the people of Connecticut were unconstitutionally outlawing the sale of contraceptives, because — it imagined — in the "penumbras" of the Constitution there is a right to privacy that prohibits that policy.[22] Penumbras? What total and complete nonsense. The justices made a policy choice and then made something up in the Constitution to effectuate it. Now you may well agree with dissenting justice Potter Stewart that the statute was "an uncommonly silly law," but we should all agree with him that it was nevertheless constitutional.

It was, of course, no great surprise that eight years later the Court found that this "right to privacy" extends to the right of a woman to choose to terminate her pregnancy—a rather tepid euphemism for ending the life of the unborn baby.[23] The decision and its basis in this fictitious right were, while narrowed in at least some respects, upheld in *Planned Parenthood v. Casey* in 1995. In what can only be described as an arrogant commitment to itself— an ode to its own legitimacy, if you will—the Court actually touted its self-given "authority to decide [the people's] constitutional cases and speak before all others for their constitutional ideals." I assume the Court would like us to say thank you, but I also assume that the 52 million or so unborn children who never had a shot at the American dream may beg to differ.[24]

That the issue is a difficult one and invokes strong emotion makes it no less outrageous that nine unelected judges took it upon themselves to declare when life begins and did so based on a total fiction. And perhaps worst of all, the Court's creation of a right to privacy in the Constitution has become a springboard for even more activism.

Our Ability to Define Marriage

Leave it to the modern liberal to take an institution that has served as the bedrock of civilization for thousands of years and find a way to make it controversial. Yet that is what we see today. Indeed, I believe that in the next five years, the United States Supreme Court will rule that it is unconstitutional to recognize marriage as only between one man and one woman.

Shouldn't such a fundamental issue about the moral ordering of society be determined by the people themselves? Of course it should — if you have any respect for the Constitution, federalism, or freedom. Yet, the Court has already set the stage for *its* policy choice. And, not surprisingly, we Texans were at the center of the issue at hand. In 2003, the Supreme Court heard the case of two homosexual men who had been arrested and convicted under a Texas law that prohibited the act of sodomy.[25] Reversing its decision from seventeen years earlier (upholding a Georgia ban), the Court found a right to homosexual sodomy. Justice Kennedy explained why by digging back into a special concurrence from the *Casey* decision upholding abortion when he wrote, "At the heart of liberty is the right to define one's own concept of existence, of meaning, of the universe, and of the mystery of human life."[26]

I don't even know what that means, but it certainly has nothing to do with the Constitution or the law. As Judge Bork said of it, "That is not an argument but a Sixties oration. It has no discernible intellectual content; it does not even tell us why the right to define one's own concept of 'meaning' includes a right to abortion or homosexual sodomy but not a right to incest, prostitution, embezzlement, or anything else."[27] But the real concern lies with the direction the Court clearly wishes to take the nation yet refuses to admit. Justice Scalia explained in dissent:

> One of the benefits of leaving regulation of this matter to the people...is that the people, unlike judges, need not carry things to their logical conclusion. The people may feel that their disapprobation of homosexual conduct is strong enough to disallow homosexual marriage, but not strong enough to criminalize private homosexual acts — and may legislate accordingly. The Court today pretends that...we need not

fear judicial imposition of homosexual marriage.... Do not believe it.[28]

Was Justice Scalia correct? Of course he was. Consider that less than eight months later, the Massachusetts Supreme Court struck down that state's ban on homosexual marriage.[29] There have been numerous such rulings since, including in early 2010 when a federal district judge in Massachusetts struck down significant parts of the federal Defense of Marriage Act. Even former Republican solicitor general Ted Olson is representing a challenge in federal court to Proposition 8, passed by the people of California in 2008 limiting marriage to one man and one woman.

Gay marriage will soon be the policy of the United States, irrespective of federalism, the Constitution, or the wishes of the American people. Not because it actually is protected in the Constitution, but because judges will declare it so.

Our Ability to Stop "Divvying Us Up by Race"

Chief Justice John Roberts had one of the best lines I can remember from a Supreme Court justice, because it succinctly captured my view of race relations in our country. In *LULAC v. Perry* (yes, I am "Perry"), a case challenging how Texas had drawn the lines for congressional districts after the 2000 Census, he wrote, "It's a sordid business, this divvying us up by race."[30] This simple sentence acknowledged the reality that we are using the very tools we created for the purpose of ending racial discrimination to perpetuate it.

I am (thankfully) not a lawyer, but the issues really aren't complicated. In that 2006 case, despite a challenge to the whole statewide redistricting plan, the Supreme Court held that only one of the congressional districts Texas had drawn was in violation of the Voting Rights Act. That was the district held then by Henry Bonilla, a Hispanic Republican. The Court stunningly ruled that while the district was drawn to be "majority minority," it was not Hispanic *enough* for Hispanics to elect their "candidate of choice."[31] It was this flawed reasoning that caused the chief justice to query during arguments of the plaintiff's attorney, "What number of minority voters is just right to make a district qualify as 'Hispanic-opportunity,' rather than one masquerading as such?[32] She did not have a good answer.

I had always thought that the Voting Rights Act served to ensure that minorities, and in particular that blacks, were able to vote freely. But while politics has always caused the formation of odd-shaped districts due to so-called gerrymandering, the Voting Rights Act has now become, in effect, federally mandated and judicially enforced gerrymandering on the basis of race.

Even more, it is being used to tell each state how it can function at the most basic level, lest it violate the Voting Rights Act. Did you know that anytime the people of Texas want to move a voting booth from, say, one school to another down the street, it must get approval from the Department of Justice? That is so because Congress passed "temporary" provisions more than forty years ago to ensure compliance but has unconstitutionally extended those provisions repeatedly since that time, including most recently in 2006 for an unbelievable 25 years.

The core provisions of the Voting Rights Act are among the most important legislation ever enacted. Like the Civil Rights Act, it reflects the realization of the principles of the Declaration of Independence and, if applied correctly, should lead America forward in such a way that we truly will not be judged by the color of our skin. Unfortunately, as is true with school busing, affirmative action, and other race-based policies, that is neither how the Court nor Congress currently sees it.

*　　*　　*

The examples I have offered are just a few of the many intrusions into decisions that are not only best left to the people and the states but are constitutionally left to them. There are countless others that are equally arrogant and frustrating. For example, in 1996, after the U.S. Department of Justice sued Virginia to challenge the all-male admissions policy at the Virginia Military Institute, the Court struck down a policy that had been in place for some 157 years.[33] The Court has censored actual political free speech such as campaign contributions, while confusing obscenity with that protected right.[34] And, almost unbelievably, the Court even managed to squeeze time in to its busy activist schedule to dictate the rules of golf when in 2001 it ruled that the PGA Tour must allow Casey Martin to use a golf cart in competition. There is seemingly no end to what the Court fancies itself expert about.

Any student of American history, or even the casual observer of the news of the day, must admit that the Court adheres to the Constitution in appearance only and as a matter of necessity, finding in it or in previous case law the single nugget around which the Court can marginally justify its policy choice to keep up the pretense of actually caring one iota about the Constitution in the first place.

This idea is well explained by University of Texas law professor Lino Graglia. That the Constitution is irrelevant to the Court's decisions, he says, can be seen "in almost any of the Court's interventions in the political process." He continues:

> Consider, for example, that there was a time when the assignment of children to public schools on the basis of race was constitutionally permissible, a time when it was constitutionally prohibited, and a time, the present, when it is sometimes constitutionally required. That covers all the possibilities,

yet in all that time, the Constitution was not amended in any relevant respect. An impartial observer would have no trouble concluding that the Constitution is not the operative variable.[35]

The operative variable is nothing more than the whim of the Court, which depends on the prevailing winds of the day, often for a single judge. As I have shown, there has been one constant theme, win or lose—the fact that many decisions are slim 5–4 majorities. Indeed, the infamous swing vote on the Court, such as Justice Kennedy or, formerly, Justice O'Connor, has an incomprehensible amount of power. And for that reason, the difference between living free and not living free can come down to the whim of one justice.

It is no wonder then that there is such importance placed on each President's choices for lifetime appointments to the Supreme Court. After all, Americans are condemned to live their lives according to the policy choices of the Court without recourse, and many of these justices serve for decades. Justice John Paul Stevens, for example, served on the Court for more than 35 years. For those who do not believe that elections matter —I give you the United States Supreme Court.

We know one thing for certain about President Obama's two confirmed nominees to the Court, justices Elena Kagan and Sonia Sotomayor—they are young, committed activists who stand to reshape the Court for years to come. How do we know this? Well, consider one example regarding Justice Sotomayor, who during her 2009 hearings claimed fidelity to the *Heller* precedent recognizing an individual right to bear arms. What happens in 2010 when the *McDonald* case regarding that individual right came before the Court? She voted with her three liberal, activist colleagues against it.

Meanwhile, Justice Kagan might as well have jumped up and down shouting she is an activist during her confirmation hearing. Be it international law, the basis behind *Brown v. Board of Education,* or her answers to questions from senator Tom Coburn regarding the Commerce Clause, which she essentially refused to acknowledge any limit to, she clearly follows the mold of her mentor, Justice Thurgood Marshall, who famously said, "Do what you think is right and let the law catch up."

The current Court is considered by some a conservative court. I do not accept that. What we really have are four justices who believe in the Constitution (Roberts, Scalia, Thomas, and Alito), four justices who are committed to making policy from the bench regardless of the Constitution (Ginsburg, Breyer, Sotomayor, and Kagan), and one justice who wakes up each day basking in the glow of his power to swing the Court (Kennedy).

This is not how it should be. The Court should be revered as the guardian of the rule of law and of our most basic founding principles. It should be particularly protective of our founding structure—a unique structure of dual sovereigns that placed power as close to the people as was practical so that the people could govern themselves. Yet instead, the Court too often chooses to take it upon itself to govern and to develop policy. This is the freedom of modern America, where democracy and federalism are trumped by nine unelected judges who tell us how to live.

7

The Federal Government Fiddles: Ignoring National Security, Immigration, and the Enumerated Powers

> *Another not unimportant consideration is that the powers of the general government will be, and indeed must be, principally employed upon external objects, such as war, peace, negotiations with foreign powers, and foreign commerce.*
>
> — JOSEPH STORY, *COMMENTARIES ON THE CONSTITUTION*, 1833[1]

AS THE SAYING GOES, a jack of all trades is a master of none. The Constitution commits to the federal government the solemn responsibility for keeping our nation, and our citizens, safe from threats foreign and domestic. That is its primary function. But, because the federal government has inserted itself into so many aspects of our lives and into so many domestic responsibilities entrusted by the Founders to the states, it can no longer focus on the very duties assigned to it under the Constitution.

These duties could not be clearer in the text of the Constitution. Article I, Section 8, contains multiple grants of authority to the national government concerning defense, including the powers to "lay and collect Taxes, Duties, Imposts and Excises, to . . . Provide for the common Defence," to "declare War," "To raise and support Armies," and "To provide and maintain a Navy." Article II, of course, empowers the President as the commander in chief and gives him the power to negotiate treaties subject to the approval of the Senate.

The enumerated responsibilities of the federal government extend to other areas as well, such as immigration and naturalization, among other things. These also remain unattended to in the face of a federal government suffering from an egregious case of mission creep. The federal government's lack of focus on its appropriate—and *constitutional*—responsibilities weakens the rule of law and makes the nation less secure.

Border Security and Immigration

One of Washington's greatest failures has been its unwillingness to secure our nation's border. Reasonable folks can disagree on many issues regarding immigration policy generally, but border security cannot be held hostage to another failed attempt at solving, in one fell swoop, all the problems of our immigration system. Our broken borders put lives at risk. They make a mockery of the rule of law.

The situation is most acute at our southern borders, where a vicious war is being conducted by terrorists of a different but equally dangerous type. In the summer of 2010, six bullets fired in Juárez, Mexico, flew across the border and struck City Hall in El Paso, Texas.[2] In August 2010, a bullet from a shoot-out in Juárez also struck the front door of Bell Hall on the campus of the University of Texas at El Paso.[3] Juárez is the site of a turf war between the Sinaloa and Juárez drug cartels, which has resulted in over 5,500 murders between January 2008 and August 2010, making it the murder capital of the world.[4] Besides the obvious drug violence, there is a disgusting undertone to all of this, marked by the murder of hundreds of women in violent sexual assaults believed by some to be carried out by prominent officials in Juárez.[5]

The driving force behind the violent cartels, of course, is narcotics, and the impact on America, and Texas, is significant. According to the U.S. State Department, roughly 90 percent of the cocaine consumed in the United States flows through Mexico from its origins in South America.[6] Between 40 and 60 percent of illegal drugs from Mexico are smuggled across a 300-mile stretch from New Mexico to Texas, including Big Bend National Park.[7] To suggest that these cartels are not terrorists, as some do, is to ignore what is actually happening. One journalist observed the rawness of the violence; a man dumped at the side of the road in the fetal position; a run of days with 10, 13, and 22 killings; a corpse hanging from an overpass; a body slumped in the driver's seat with the severed head resting on the hood; and numerous other violent images.[8]

But this terrorist activity among cartels is prevalent in other regions of Mexico, too. After the July 2010 arrests in San Diego of individuals involved in a Tijuana drug cartel, the *Los Angeles Times* wrote, "Federal authorities announced a wide-ranging criminal case Friday against top leaders of a Tijuana-based drug cartel that ran much of its operations from the San Diego area, allegedly ordering murders, kidnappings and the torture of rival traffickers in Mexico."[9] More than 28,200 people have been killed across Mexico since 2007, when President Felipe Calderón escalated his efforts against the cartels.[10]

And the violence doesn't stop there. It is extending up into the United States. In Pinal County, Arizona, there has been violence along a smuggling route as far as 70 miles north of the border. In April 2010, a Pinal County sheriff's deputy was shot by an illegal alien carrying an AK-47 rifle.[11] It's so dangerous down there that some 3,500 acres of a national wildlife refuge—public land owned by Americans—is closed to American citizens. The Pinal County sheriff is receiving death threats because of his efforts to combat the flow of illegal immigration and smuggling, as well as for his support for stepped-up enforcement. And there have been countless examples of the spillover into my state of Texas. Consider just some I have been made aware of as governor:

- In 2008 in Del Rio, Texas, there were six bomb threats.
- A hand grenade was thrown by a cartel member into a bar in Pharr, Texas, likely targeting off-duty law enforcement officers inside.
- Border Patrol agents working near Laredo were pinned down by gunfire from the Mexico side of the Rio Grande River. With the assistance of Laredo PD and other Border Patrol agents, the two agents were rescued.
- A shoot-out in Matamoros between cartel members and the Mexican military resulted in the shutdown of the University of Texas campus at Brownsville because of bullets hitting the campus grounds.
- A Horizon City, Texas, man was kidnapped from his home in front of his family and found murdered six days later in Mexico, with his severed arms crossed over his chest.

Federal authorities repeatedly promise to start protecting Americans from the violence. But, El Paso police chief Greg Allen says, "The Feds fly out, and we never hear from them again, and it's getting a little bit old. Quite frankly, if a U.S. citizen is killed due to the neglect of the federal government, then something is wrong with the big picture."[12] I agree with Chief Allen. The federal government talks seriously about the southern border and the increased lawlessness in Mexico, but it must get serious. So far, however, the federal government's actions fall somewhere between raging incompetence and outright dereliction of duty.

The brutality is also, in part, an outgrowth of a serious effort by President Calderón to shut down the corruption and violence of powerful cartels. Never before have we had such a strong partner in Mexico's highest office. He has disarmed entire police departments corrupted by drug money, and sent in soldiers and federal law enforcement to trouble spots. He is waging all-out war against narcoterrorists who have operated with impunity on both sides of the border. Now is the time to step up our support, to be a real partner by enhancing the security of the border and bringing all resources to bear in this fight.

Border security, unfortunately, has been unnecessarily and inappropriately wrapped up with "comprehensive immigration." Before I get into the specifics of this problem, let me be clear that, just like my fellow Texans, I am very much in favor of legal immigration and am proud of our diverse heritage in this country. In fact, the United States opens its front doors to more than 1 million people each year. People around the world recognize the opportunities available here because of our historic belief in free markets and individual responsibility, and we have a long tradition of welcoming with open arms those who want to come here and build a better life.

Texans in particular enjoy a unique culture that has been greatly enriched by immigrants from all over the world, and especially from Mexico. Our history is steeped in the unique melding of Mexican and Anglo cultures. We are proud of that history and embrace it—from our music and our food to our culture generally. Yet this has absolutely nothing to do with border security. We can have all the immigration debates we want, but Americans are demanding that the border be secured first.

We have already been burned once by false promises of border security in exchange for tying security to other aspects of the immigration debate. President Reagan, in 1986, signed the Immigration Reform and Control Act, which legalized close to 3 million undocumented immigrants.[13] The law was supposed to be a comprehensive solution with provisions intended to clamp down on border security. These provisions were never enforced, and the subsequent explosion in illegal crossings has resulted in some 11 million illegal aliens living in the United States today.[14] An estimated 1.8 million illegal immigrants are currently residing in Texas, compared with 1.1 million in 2000. In ten years, that represents an increase of 54 percent, or 70,000 persons each year coming to our state illegally.[15] Today, the Pew Hispanic Center estimates that about one in ten people born in Mexico live in the United States.[16] And all of this has occurred outside the system and to the disadvantage of others who have been waiting in line for many years. There are literally millions of people waiting to get into the country legally.

These levels of unchecked illegal immigration are unsustainable. We expend vast resources on illegal immigrants and our own security. State and local governments, which provide essential services like schooling and emergency health care to illegal immigrants, often under a mandate from the federal courts, bear the brunt of the immense fiscal burden. A 2007 study by the Congressional Budget Office reached several conclusions relevant to this issue. Among them, the CBO pointed out that while most of the welfare or public assistance programs operated by the federal government, like Social Security, food stamps, and Temporary Assistance for Needy Families, are not available to illegal immigrants, the same federal government requires states to provide certain benefits to illegal immigrants in order for states to participate in programs receiving federal funds.[17] Education is a good example. Emergency medical care is another. Any health care facility receiving federal funds must provide certain care even for individuals who cannot pay for it, including many illegal immigrants.

A 2006 report by the Texas comptroller's office estimated the budgetary impacts of illegal immigration in Texas. The report found that approximately 135,000 undocumented students in Texas public schools cost the state $957 million in just the 2004–2005 school year.[18] Other studies using different population estimates and including federal spending have pointed to even higher costs of $1.2 billion (for the 2004–2005 school year) and $1.7 billion (for the 2003–2004 school year). The comptroller's report cited incarceration and uncompensated health care as the two largest costs associated with illegal immigrants to local government entities in Texas. These two items cost local governments $1.44 billion over a one-year period.

Of course, those living in Texas illegally also provide income to the state because of increased economic activity, sales taxes, and property taxes (either directly or through rent subsidizing the property owner). But adding the estimated revenues and costs to both the state and local governments, Texas taxpayers were out $928 million in 2005.[19]

The State Criminal Alien Assistance Program (SCAAP) is a case study in the refusal of the federal government to do its job at our borders. SCAAP was created in 1994 to reimburse states for part of the cost of incarcerating illegal immigrants who commit crimes.

Naturally, however, SCAAP is more window dressing than real policy, as it is woefully underfunded. A study commissioned by the United States/Mexico Border Counties Coalition found that in 2006, border counties in California, Arizona, New Mexico, and Texas on the Mexican border received a total of only $4.7 million in SCAAP reimbursements, representing 9 percent of the costs of handling illegal immigrants who committed state crimes.[20] Among just those border counties in Texas, the reimbursement rate was a mere 3 percent.[21] The reimbursement rate is so low that some counties do not even apply for funding because it is not worth the cost of paperwork.[22]

This is a joke. Arizona governor Jan Brewer has calculated that her state alone is owed $700 million in SCAAP funds since 2003.[23] Former Arizona governor Janet Napolitano wrote in 2008 that "as governor, I must enforce the law and pay to incarcerate these individuals. The federal government just shrugs its shoulders and walks away from its statutory obligation."[24] Now serving as President Obama's Secretary of Homeland Security, she has not persuaded the federal government to step up to the plate.

The bottom line is that while our federal officials jealously claim exclusive authority over immigration and border policy, they avoid actually securing the border. While they mandate that state taxpayers provide services, they rarely confront any of the associated costs.[25] In so doing, the federal government refuses to fulfill its most basic constitutional responsibilities.

A grand, bipartisan compromise on immigration similar to the failed 1986 law was attempted in both 2006 and 2007. In the end, the bill died, largely because the American people had been to this rodeo before. According to an ABC News poll taken in the heat of the debate in 2007, two-thirds of Americans did not believe Congress was serious about controlling illegal immigration.[26]

Now, the current administration willfully refuses to enforce the laws on the books. While President Bush didn't do as much as I had hoped, his administration did step up workplace enforcement, reducing the enticement for illegal immigration. President

Obama, on the other hand, has reversed course.[27] He also has intentionally undermined one of the few successful measures the federal government has implemented. Section 287(g) of the Immigration and Nationality Act allows the "deputization" of local law enforcement after training from federal authorities so that they may process illegal immigrants detained in the course of law enforcement activities for removal. This program simply allows local officials to aid Immigration and Customs Enforcement in the application of our laws.

Bowing to pressure from interest groups in favor of unchecked illegal immigration, the Obama administration has instead issued new requirements intended to curtail the program by making it more expensive, among other things.[28] So the federal government is now manipulating successful programs to stop willing local jurisdictions from doing the federal government's job themselves.

The security and public safety implications of this decision are serious. In Houston in 2006, officer Rodney Johnson was gunned down by an illegal alien he had stopped on a routine traffic violation. The alien, Juan Leonardo Quintero, had been convicted previously of indecency with a child and driving while intoxicated, and was deported in 2004.[29] Of course, he easily reentered the country and later committed this heinous crime. But Johnson was not the only Houston officer to be shot as a result of lax border enforcement. In March 2009, an illegal alien shot officer Rick Salter, who, thankfully, survived; and in June 2009, another Houston officer, Henry Canales, was killed by an illegal alien.[30] These are just a few examples of many.

The federal government fails us in every facet of its immigration policy. The visa and naturalization system is not working efficiently for anybody — not for foreign individuals looking for opportunities or for American businesses that would like to temporarily fill specialized jobs.[31] Our immigration court system is overburdened, understaffed, and hopelessly backlogged. There were 602,000 unenforced deportation orders in 2002, and 558,000 of them remained unenforced six years later.[32]

President Obama is now trying to do just enough to create the impression of some activity to address border security. He announced that he will send 1,200 National Guard troops to the border, as a temporary measure, until an additional 1,000 Border Patrol agents are on the job.[33] This has generated headlines — and I suppose it is better than the alternative of no additional troops or officers — but it is really a drop in the bucket. Consider that of those 1,200 troops, only 286 were assigned to Texas.[34] The southern border of the United States stretches 1,954 miles, and 1,255 of them are in Texas.[35] We have 60 percent of the border, yet less than 25 percent of the resources were given to Texas to deal with it. In the face of the soaring violence infesting our border communities as a result of the drug trade, this paltry effort is simply inviting more problems.

When the citizens of Arizona decided that they could no longer wait for the federal government, they passed a law aimed at increasing the security of their communities. Other states and municipalities have likewise passed legislation to do the job the federal government refuses to do. What was Washington's response to our sister state's SOS? It sued Arizona and complained we will get a "patchwork" of immigration enforcement. The federal government's argument amounts to this: the feds have exclusive authority over immigration policy, whether or not they enforce the laws on the books. Arizona's enforcement of immigration laws interferes with this federal policy of total abdication and is therefore preempted.

Yet states and local communities have a duty to protect the safety of their citizens and, moreover, a long-settled right to facilitate enforcement of federal law. The longer the feds sit idly by, the more localities that will follow with measures similar to Arizona's.

A patchwork is exactly what we will have all over this country until the federal government finally decides to step up to the plate and address our border security problems.

"Common Defence"

We currently have tens of thousands of courageous servicemen and -women in Iraq and Afghanistan. Their mission in these countries and others is critical to our safety here at home, and it must be the absolute priority of our national government to ensure their success. Like all wars, these are complicated, dangerous engagements, and we need representatives in Washington who will focus on them.

We are also now confronted with the rise of new economic and military powerhouses in China and India, as well as a Russia that is increasingly aggressive and troublesome to its neighbors and the former satellite nations that are struggling to maintain their relatively newfound independence. There is no reason to believe that armed conflict with any major power is imminent, but the world is rapidly changing, and the United States must be prepared for the ramifications of shifting balances of power.

North Korea and Iran, in contrast, are utterly unpredictable and do present an imminent threat with their nuclear ambitions. Kim Jong-il's regime recently sunk a South Korean ship, the *Cheonan,* for no apparent reason, killing 46 sailors. The United Nations responded with its characteristic force, passing yet another resolution expressing displeasure. Iran is rattling its sabers and developing nuclear technology with impunity. Leftists in Latin America are threatening democracy, and Hugo Chávez is harboring communist rebels in Venezuela. All of these issues require our attention and investment in defense capabilities.

Yet it is clear that after decades of ignoring the constitutional division of authority, our bloated national government is distracted and running thin on resources to perform its central mission. It is true that spending on defense has increased since September 11, 2001, particularly when the costs associated with Iraq and Afghanistan are included. However, even accounting for Iraq and Afghanistan, the Pentagon's 2011 budget request, at slightly more than $700 billion, is 4.8 percent of gross domestic product, a level below the historical average for defense spending.[36]

Even so, defense spending is now being squeezed out of the budget because of the explosion in entitlement spending. Secretary of Defense Robert Gates sounded the alarms in May 2010. Citing "America's difficult economic circumstances and parlous fiscal condition," Gates warned that "military spending on things large and small can and should expect closer scrutiny."[37] While he was deliberately circumspect regarding the causes of our country's problems, as an honorable member of the President's cabinet must be, the verdict is clear—the unsustainable fiscal wreck created after decades of Washington run amok is now threatening the government's paramount security function. Gates said that he cannot even count on maintaining current forces:

> The fact that we are a nation at war and facing an uncertain world, I believe, calls for sustaining the current military force structure—Army brigades, Marine regiments, Air Force wings, Navy ships. This typically requires regular real growth in the defense budget ranging from two and three percent above inflation.... But, realistically, it is highly unlikely that we will achieve the real growth rates necessary to sustain the current force structure.[38]

While the entitlement state expands, the discretionary spending controlled by Congress each year, which includes defense spending, is becoming an ever smaller part of the budget. The Congressional Budget Office has said that by 2017, interest on the national debt will cost more than the entire defense budget.[39] And this lack of focus on the defense function has already resulted in pressing problems.

The Air Force provides some striking examples. Our air fleet needs serious attention if we are to maintain our air superiority. For years the Pentagon has wanted to replace its aging fleet of tankers, some of which have been in service since the Eisenhower administration.[40] The cockpit of one tanker in use in Afghanistan is in such a state that the pilot told a reporter, "It's absolutely amazing it stays in the air still."[41] The Air Force spends $1.8 billion every year on upkeep for these tankers, as the contract for new planes has been delayed due to a significantly flawed procurement system.[42]

Don't doubt that as more countries acquire sophisticated air-defense capabilities, our military capabilities will be seriously curtailed if we do not move forward with the next generation of fighter jets, most of which are slated to be the F-35 Joint Strike Fighter. Michael Wynne, former secretary of the Air Force, has said that "For any country with a decent air defense system, we'll need F-35s. There's no fighter alternative."[43] However, the F-35 program is in jeopardy due to higher-than-anticipated costs. Secretary Gates has also announced cuts to the Air Force's planned fleet of F-22 fighter jets and the Army's Future Combat Systems, both of which were slated to be central components of military modernization plans. Lest the Navy feel excluded from the chopping block, Gates also warned that "fiscal realities will preclude the Navy from reaching its goal of 313 ships."

Washington's lack of focus on the fundamental defense mission is manifesting itself in other ways. President Obama's 2010 Quadrennial Defense Review (QDR), the periodic strategic plan for our national defense, devoted a full three pages to climate change, mentioning it more times than China, Russia, North Korea, or Iran.[44] And, nuclear policy has also veered badly off track. President Obama's heavily reported Prague speech in April 2009 contained this sentence: "I state clearly and with conviction America's commitment to seek the peace and security of a world without nuclear weapons."[45] He goes on to cite several "concrete steps" the United States will take to achieve this utter fantasy, one of which is to secure a new treaty that "verifiably ends the production of fissile materials intended for use in ... nuclear weapons."

We don't need a stable of U.N. lawyers to tell us that the international system has no reliable mechanism for enforcing such a treaty. Inevitably, any number of rogue countries would be (and are) able to produce a nuclear weapon under the noses of inspectors. David Kay, the leader of the U.N. inspections team that discovered Iraq's nuclear program after the first Gulf War, wrote recently, "The blunt truth is that weapons inspections simply cannot prevent a government in charge of a large country from developing nuclear weapons, when that government has decided to breach its obligations not to."[46] The pursuit of such a policy is naive and dangerous because you cannot put the nuclear cat back in the bag. It's as if we learned nothing from the Reagan era, in particular the notion of peace through strength. Ridding the world of nuclear weapons may appease the most ardent leftist protestors, but it ignores the realities of a world full of power-hungry despots who respect us not because of our ideals but because of our strength.

CIA director Leon Panetta said on June 27, 2010, that within two years, Iran could have nuclear weapons.[47] By 2015, the fanatic ayatollahs in charge of that country may be able to build an intercontinental ballistic missile capable of reaching the U.S. East Coast.[48] Sanctions passed by Congress this year will not solve this problem. Referring to the sanctions, Panetta said, "Will it deter them from their ambitions with regards to nuclear policy? Probably not."[49]

Former CIA director James Woolsey lays out these facts in a recent commentary on the importance of the continued development of our missile defense system. He warns that under the current plan, which scrapped the Bush administration's plan for more capable sites in the Czech Republic and Poland, we would not have robust protection for the U.S. homeland until 2020. "That's almost certainly too late," Woolsey says. "The Obama administration should re-evaluate its missile defense strategy."[50] "Above all," Woolsey continues, the administration "should clarify to the U.S. Senate and the Russian government that neither the New START [see below] nor commitments made during the negotiation process will in any way limit our ability to protect ourselves against an Iranian nuclear attack."[51]

And the effect was more than just strategic — it was a slap in the face to a number of our allies. As a *Wall Street Journal* article put it, "Some prominent figures in the region, such as former Polish President Lech Walesa, worried the new U.S. administration was turning away from its traditional allies in Central Europe to placate Russia."[52] But there is good news for those who prefer our foreign policy be popular among the European elite, because NATO's secretary general, Anders Fogh Rasmussen, welcomed the U.S. policy shift, saying it was his "clear impression that the American plan on missile defense will involve NATO…to a higher degree in the future."[53] Surely we can't be serious?

Woolsey refers to a new United States–Russia nuclear arms reduction treaty. Dubbed New START, the pact would set a lower ceiling on the number of nuclear weapons applicable to both countries. It has been criticized by serious observers for, among other things, allowing the Russians to build its arsenal while requiring that we tear ours down (the Russians currently have fewer warheads than the treaty would allow).[54] Republican members of the Senate have noted several problems with the treaty that could undermine our security and have pleaded that it be taken off the fast track until they receive more information from the State Department.

Nothing is more critical to the welfare of our nation nor more fundamental to the powers granted to the federal government than our national security. Yet, the current regime treats it like some international popularity contest while focusing its time on countless matters not remotely contemplated for federal action by the Founders.

NASA and Space

President Obama has made similarly naive and dangerous proclamations regarding space policy. He seems intent on effectively dismantling NASA and our space program. NASA captured the nation's imagination when President Kennedy boldly announced the ambitious space race, and we beat the Russians to the moon. But, unlike President Kennedy, President Obama seems more inclined to turn NASA into a Muslim outreach effort than to advance our interests in space.

In comments that created a firestorm of disbelief, the current NASA administrator, Charles Bolden, said in an interview with Al Jazeera that the President had given him three objectives; "Perhaps foremost, he wanted me to find a way to reach out to the Muslim world and engage much more with dominantly Muslim nations to help them feel good about their historic contribution to science...and math and engineering."[55] Meanwhile, NASA's next-generation space-exploration program is in danger of being halted by this administration in direct contradiction to the express wishes of Congress.[56] This while ending the space shuttle program at the same time, rendering the United States entirely dependent on the international community—most especially Russia—for our near-term space activity, on which so much of our national security and economy depend.

Intelligence and Counterterrorism

The *Washington Post* recently ran a series of articles summing up a two-year investigation into the post-9/11 national security framework. Its central conclusion: "The system...is so massive that its effectiveness is impossible to determine."[57] The reporters counted 1,271 government organizations and 1,931 private companies engaged in "counterterrorism, homeland security and intelligence" functions in 10,000 locations in the United States. Retired lieutenant general John R. Vines was quoted as saying that because the system is not synchronized, "it inevitably results in message dissonance, reduced effectiveness and waste," and that "we can't effectively assess whether it is making us more safe."[58]

The best candidates for the job of director of national intelligence have refused the position because of the uncertainty surrounding the DNI's authority over the various parts of the intelligence community and the difficulty of operating in the current framework. Dennis Blair resigned the position in May 2010 in the wake of several intelligence failures related to the Fort Hood attack, the underwear bomber, and the attempted Times Square car bombing.[59] Blair was a capable and respected public servant, but widespread reports point to turf battles between his office, the CIA, and the White House, which have harmed our intelligence efforts. While the Office of the Director of National

Intelligence was constructed in order to coordinate the intelligence community, obvious problems persist.

Secretary of Defense Robert Gates and CIA director Leon Panetta both acknowledged that serious problems remain. The failure to prevent Umar Farouk Abdulmutallab, the so-called underwear bomber, from boarding a plane with a bomb strapped to his body is a case in point. Several pieces of information, including a warning from Abdulmutallab's father, made their way to various intelligence analysts. As Blair later testified, "Everyone had the dots to connect. But I hadn't made it clear exactly who had primary responsibility."[60]

Almost a full decade after the attacks of September 11, 2001, Washington still has not settled on a policy for detaining and, if necessary, prosecuting enemies captured in the War on Terror. President Obama naively campaigned as if terrorism should be handled as a law enforcement matter, and in November 2009 Attorney General Holder held a major press conference to announce that Guantanamo Bay would be shuttered and that 9/11 mastermind Khalid Sheikh Mohammed would face a civilian trial in Manhattan.[61] Both plans have crumbled in the face of public and congressional opposition, and to this day the administration refuses to decide what to do. Washington's paralysis on the seminal issue of our time — dealing with terrorists whose mission is to kill as many Americans as possible — signals weakness to our enemies.

Washington simply cannot follow basic instructions. The Constitution is not a complicated document. The federal government's core function is to defend the nation. Yet our military is strained, our leaders are more concerned about world popularity than strength, and our borders remain porous.

Moreover, it's failing at its other enumerated powers as well. Congress has power to "regulate Commerce with foreign nations," yet three trade agreements negotiated by the Bush administration have languished for years in a congressional dead zone due to opposition, mainly from liberal Democrats afraid of alienating their union supporters.

The federal government also has the express power to "promote the Progress of Science and useful Arts" by issuing patents, but it has failed to keep pace with rapidly changing technology and business innovation.[62] Without clear rules of the road, businesses must shoulder extra costs from litigation over property rights, and the consumer misses out.

I could go on. While spending countless hours taking over banks, automakers, and health care, managing charity, bickering over the philosophical aspects of immigration, inserting itself into education, and so on, the federal government is stretched thin, so thin that it is proving itself incapable of handling even those narrow functions that it constitutionally is required to perform.

8

Standing Athwart History Not Doing a Damned Thing

*It is natural for man to indulge in the illusions of hope.
We are apt to shut our eyes against a painful truth, and
listen to the song of that siren till she transforms us into
beasts. Is this the part of wise men, engaged in a great
and arduous struggle for liberty?*

— PATRICK HENRY, SPEECH TO VIRGINIA CONVENTION,
MARCH 23, 1775[1]

WHEN THE GREAT William F. Buckley founded the
National Review, he said famously in the first issue that the magazine "stands athwart history, yelling Stop, at a time when no one
is inclined to do so."[2] He recognized that for something bad to be
stopped, someone has to be willing to fight it. But sadly, and for
too long, no one has been.

Our primary lines of defense against the tyranny of an expansive and meddlesome federal government are the states. But
because Washington is unconstrained by a Supreme Court that
largely ignores the Tenth Amendment and principles of federalism, we are left hoping that Republicans in Washington will actually fight for a limited, constitutional government. And therein
lies a problem.

For all the great efforts of Buckley and those conservatives who followed in his footsteps, from Barry Goldwater to President Ronald Reagan, where do we stand today? Is government any smaller? Are markets freer? Are states more empowered? Perhaps I suppose that relative to what might have been, the answer is "sort of"—but as we have seen in the preceding chapters, in actual terms the answer is a resounding "no." Government is as large as it has ever been and growing by the second. The markets are under assault by too many bailouts and takeovers to count. And the powers specifically designed to remain with the states, and the people, are being trampled.

While the modern Democrat is unabashedly committed to expanding the federal government and willing to wake up every day fighting to do it, the average Republican too often shows up to the fight seeking something "less bad" than what the Democrat wants. That's not a fight, it's a concession. Tomorrow will come and the Democrat will be on the battlefield again, expecting the Republican to once again capitulate—and, unfortunately, he would be correct.

Republicans today prefer to use government to achieve their own preferred, supposedly conservative, policy goals and give lip service to the idea of limiting it overall. The idea seems to be that if the federal government is increased less than the Democrats want, then Republicans have done the best they can. As any good psychologist will tell you, playing not to lose is very different from playing to win, and for too many years now, that is precisely what even our most "conservative" Republicans have been doing. The result is a one-sided fight.

If there is supposedly some great struggle—or ebb and flow—between the forces of centralization who seek to concentrate power in Washington and those who prefer to follow the Constitution and empower the states, why then has there never been a significant non-war-related retreat in the size and scope of the federal government? In the over 220 years since the adoption of our Constitution, wouldn't there have been at least one significant movement away from centralization? Wouldn't we see a time when many more federal laws were removed from the books than added? But when has any of that happened? It hasn't. Simply put, no one is even willing to utter the word "stop," much less yell it.

Instead, power in Washington begets more power. It's an endless cycle. Now, I am not talking about who controls which branch of government. I am talking about the *real power of control*— of spending money and playing kingmaker as a powerful committee chairman or as a powerful secretary of a department. See, those who get power simply want more of it and are willing to set aside principle to maintain it. As James Madison once noted, "All men having power ought to be distrusted to a certain degree." In this case, it is through their very empowerment that Washington continues to grow unabated and liberty is lost.[3]

The American people are starting to figure out this reality. They understand that no less than the future of the Republic is at stake even when no one in Washington seems to. Their mounting frustration with the federal government and those who run it is not driven by party loyalty or even simple cynicism, but rather by the fear that the nation they love has for too long been charting an unsustainable course and that there appears to be precious little leadership willing to change it for fear of losing power. They are fed up with a culture of corruption, failure, and incompetence in Washington that is devoid of any notion of responsibility, limited government, or sense of duty to preserve and protect the country.

As a result, the political winds of change have been blowing back and forth for several election cycles and show no signs of slowing down. The gains by Republicans in the elections of 2010 stand for a number of things, including frustration with the policies promoted by both the Obama administration and congressional Democrats. But it goes a lot deeper than that. The winds of change are focused also on Republicans who don't get it. If you doubt this, look at Republican primary results from coast to coast: in Utah, the party refused to renominate Senator Bob Bennett and instead chose upstart Mike Lee; in Florida, support for bailouts and stimulus funding was so toxic that Governor Charlie Crist gave up on seeking the Republican nomination for the U.S. Senate and instead forged an independent candidacy in plain view of imminent defeat at the hands of Marco Rubio; in Alaska, incumbent Lisa Murkowski was defeated by the more conservative Joe Miller; and among others, the young and conservative Christine O'Donnell shocked the establishment by defeating Mike Castle in Delaware. In my opinion, the state of affairs can be summed up like this: Democrats aren't close to representing the beliefs and values of most Americans, but Washington Republicans haven't been willing to stand up and fight. And that's what the people are fed up with.

Democrats Are Committed to Expanding Government

It was largely the Democrats who brought you the New Deal. It was largely the Democrats who brought you the Great Society. And it is largely the Democrats today who ride an army of steamrollers over the American people as they seek to increase the power of government. Elected Democrats, particularly on the national stage, simply no longer represent the values of the American people I know. They believe less in the people themselves than they believe in the government.

Some might suggest that this is a provocative statement. But what is provocative about speaking the truth? Reasonable people can disagree about the role of government in our lives, but let's at least be honest about the fact that Democrats long ago abandoned any sense of limited government and the role of states in guaranteeing that the people may live according to their deeply rooted American values. And that saddens me.

As I mentioned earlier, I grew up a southern New Deal Democrat. My parents were Democrats, as was virtually everyone I knew. Heck, the only election that really mattered was the Democratic primary election, not the general election. When I first ran for state office as a Republican, my home county had to do something they had never done before: conduct a Republican primary election. My party switch in 1989 was preceded by a long leftward drift by the Democratic Party. Democrats were no longer the party of Jackson and the people, but the party of Roosevelt, Kennedy, and now Obama—more interested in government and the opinions of Harvard, Washington, and Upper West Side Manhattan than the beliefs of those people in flyover country between the coasts.

Can anyone in good faith suggest that the modern Democrat does not seek to empower Washington and expand the federal government? Does the modern Democrat represent the values of you or the Americans you know? Does he, in any way, respect our nation's core founding principles of federalism and limited government? I cannot see it. Consider the following comments by Democrats:

- Did Barack Obama represent America when he referred to *"bitter working class voters cling[ing] to guns or religion"*?[4]
- Did House Speaker Nancy Pelosi demonstrate a belief in limited government when she said, *"My biggest fight has been between those who wanted to do something incremental and those who wanted to do something comprehensive.... We won that fight, and once we kick through this door, there'll be more legislation to follow"*?[5]

- Did Senator Byron Dorgan demonstrate an understanding that it's the people's money and not the government's when he said that a vote to cut taxes is a vote *"to reduce this country's income"*?[6]
- Did Congresswoman Maxine Waters represent America's belief in free markets when she said, *"Guess what this liberal would be all about? This liberal will be all about socializing...would be about basically taking over and the government running all of your companies"*?[7]
- Did Representative Phil Hare show any respect for the Constitution when he said about the health care bill, *"I don't worry about the Constitution on this"*?[8]
- Did Senator Chris Dodd show any concern for the limits of his power in Washington when he said about the financial regulation bill, *"No one will know until this is actually in place how it works"*?[9]

If that's not enough, is there any doubt after the vote to nationalize health care earlier this year? Consider that in the Senate, the vote was 60–39, strictly along party lines.[10] Not one Senate Democrat — not one — felt that the people of his state would rather not cede control of their health care to a federal bureaucrat. In the House, the vote was 219–212, with not a single Republican voting for the bill, and only 33 Democrats in very "red" districts voting against it.[11] States, and the people, have been shoved aside when it comes to your health, of all things.

But look even more closely — the supposed concern about abortion funding by the few self-described pro-life Democrats that even exist, including Representative Bart Stupak, was not much of a holdup at all. In the end, they voted for a bill that no actual proponent of life believed would prevent federal funding of abortions.[12] Guess what? In spite of a fig leaf executive order signed by President Obama, he had already approved taxpayer-funded abortions.[13] Whether you are pro-life or not, what is entirely clear is that there apparently are no Democrats willing to stand on that principle.

For me, it simply is not possible to conclude today that the modern Democrat believes in limited government. Rather, today's Democrat is the modern incarnation of the very "history" against which Mr. Buckley so ably and courageously stood athwart, yelling "Stop."

Washington Republicans Are Unwilling to Truly Fight

Who, pray tell, is yelling "Stop" today?

It sure isn't Washington Republicans. Now, don't misunderstand me—these days, I believe there is generally no question about which party to support. I am a proud, albeit frustrated, Republican. I am frustrated because Republicans have so often been part of the problem in Washington, rather than standing on principle to give voice to the American people. We should not endeavor to be better than Democrats only by default—that is, "Democrat Lite." Rather we should endeavor to demonstrate that we believe in something bigger than ourselves.

I realize I will take some heat for pointing this out. Much is made by establishment Republicans of the so-called eleventh commandment, one sentence uttered by Reagan in 1976: "Thou shalt not speak ill of any fellow Republican."[14] Well, I love and respect the Gipper as much as the next American and agree that Republicans should support one another, but he also said, "Presidents come and go. History comes and goes, but principles endure."

The truth is that in the face of a constant drumbeat to centralize power in Washington, Republicans too often either sit on the sidelines or actually make the problem worse. Sure, on a number of issues, Republicans have united to oppose bad legislation — notably the abhorrent health care legislation. But that hardly takes any courage — they're *supposed* to do that, after all. More often they choose to reach across the aisle to take the best they can get. The idea seems to be that if the federal government is increased less than the Democrats want, then Republicans should be congratulated for it. Perhaps worse than compromise, the idea of actually limiting government seems to be but a quaint notion today for Republicans who prefer instead to set aside principle to use government to achieve their own, preferred supposedly conservative — policy goals.

From my perspective, there have been three significant moments in history when there has been real hope for conservative reform in Washington and a genuine retreat in the size and scope of the federal government. The first two moments were the election of Ronald Reagan in 1980 and the Contract with America in 1994, when Republicans took control of the Senate and the House for the first time in over 40 years. Each was an important moment because, when viewed in the context of history, it sent a strong signal that the American people were fed up with the long march of government expansion. Ronald Reagan not only defeated communism, but inspired a generation of Americans — including me — to remember the rugged individualism and self-determination that made this country great.

But each also fell short of its promise of truly shifting direction back to the states and the people. During the Reagan years of the 1980s, federal spending still doubled, numerous federal agencies expanded, and there was a proliferation of federal criminal laws. Only 12 of 94 programs the administration proposed to eliminate actually ended. And programs that were "scaled back" simply returned in full force in the face of a relentless Democratic

Congress. Take for example the Small Business Administration, which was cut from $2 billion in 1980 to $85 million in 1989, but which had grown back to $975 million by the end of the first Bush administration in 1993.[15]

The Republican Revolution of 1994 was a slightly less valiant effort, resulting (mainly) in changes to a few rules, welfare reform, and some slowdown in the growth of spending. The popularity of welfare reform led to President Clinton declaring in a State of the Union address that "the era of big government is over." If only those words had actually been true, and not just a triangulation gimmick. In that case, what had been achieved in several states — especially in Governor Tommy Thompson's home state of Wisconsin and Governor John Engler's home state of Michigan — led to major federal reform that placed reasonable time constraints on benefits, among other important changes. Here we see how innovation ought to work — using the states as policy laboratories and then adopting best practices at the federal level where appropriate and within its jurisdiction.

But a number of 1994's promises went unfulfilled and most of that spending restraint came from not fighting President Clinton's efforts to cut military spending, which dropped to 3 percent of GDP, the lowest point since the beginning of World War II and well off the 6 percent mark set under President Reagan less than a decade earlier.[16] Republican control meant we were better off than we would have been with Democrats in control, but nothing fundamentally changed about how Washington works in a significant way.

The third moment came in 2000 with the election of a Republican President along with a (mostly) Republican Congress. Conservatives looked forward to the chance to finally take control of the federal government, constrain it, and to try to fix the many legacy problems of the New Deal and the Great Society, such as

Social Security. Unfortunately, none of that actually happened. The branding of Compassionate Conservatism meant that the GOP was sending the wrong signal that conservatism alone wasn't sufficient or, worse yet, was somehow flawed and had to be rebranded. For the first time, we were acting like liberals who call themselves progressives, running away to some degree from who we were, and what we stood for. The result is an ongoing, near-complete capitulation to the federal welfare state.

Let me say again as clearly as I can say it that I have enormous respect and admiration for my fellow Texan, President George W. Bush. He is a friend and a great American patriot. He was undoubtedly the right man to protect this nation from the threat of terrorism and he should be commended for it. His heart is enormous; he is an exceptional human being and an even better husband and father. We should always be so lucky as to have leaders of his caliber in charge of our nation.

But as I have said before, he did not fight for fiscal conservativism with the same fervor with which he pursued the freedom agenda in his foreign policy. He was dubbed by the Republican-friendly columnist Fred Barnes in the *Weekly Standard,* "a big government conservative."[17] I am not sure that's fair to the President or to the term conservative. There is no such thing as a "big government conservative." It is an oxymoron. I do think George is basically a conservative man who believes in God, in the greatness of America, in the protection of life, and in protecting our nation from our enemies. That's a pretty good record if you ask me. But he also seemed unwilling to fight spendthrift congressional Republicans for the sake of his larger goals. In other words, he turned a blind eye to undisciplined domestic spending while he focused on ensuring funding for a very important war against the perpetrators of terror.

Ultimately, the record is fairly unforgiving for Republicans —

particularly in Congress—who have been in power in Washington over the last decade or so. They haven't just spent our money wildly—they have blatantly ignored our core founding principles and expanded the reach of Washington into our lives while blowing a once-in-a-lifetime opportunity to restore the balance of power from Washington back to states. As George Will put it when certain folks were lamenting President Obama's bold comment to Joe the Plumber that he would "spread the wealth around":

> America can't have that, exclaimed the Republican ticket, while Republicans—whose prescription drug entitlement is the largest expansion of the welfare state since President Lyndon Johnson's Great Society gave birth to Medicare in 1965; and a majority of whom in Congress supported a lavish farm bill at a time of record profits for the less than 2 percent of the American people-cum-corporations who farm—and their administration was partially nationalizing the banking system, putting Detroit on the dole and looking around to see if some bit of what is smilingly called "the private sector" has been inadvertently left off the ever-expanding list of entities eligible for a bailout from the $1 trillion or so that is to be "spread around."[18]

Washington Republicans simply blew the opportunity to demonstrate what conservatism is all about, and why it works. And it's a shame. Consider the sheer magnitude of the following notable (of many more possible) examples, every single one of which occurred on the Republican watch during the last decade, and often with overwhelming Republican support:

• *No Child Left Behind:* This legislation is a direct assault on federalism. It increases Washington's power over the education of your children by holding billions of dollars over the heads of states to encourage them to adhere to specific testing standards and requirements. Since the inception of NCLB, federal funding of schools is up more than 40 percent.[19] In 2001, Republicans in the Senate supported the measure 43–6, and in the House, 185–34. Maybe with that great title on the bill, it was a hard one, politically, to leave behind?

• *Earmarks and Runaway Federal Spending:* Republicans of the last decade increased federal spending more than at any time since FDR, with spending growing from 33 percent of GDP in 2001 to 42 percent by 2009.[20] While military spending necessary to fight two wars and to rebuild after Clinton's cuts (with Republican acquiescence) was part of the increase, it was far from all of it. In 1994, the year before Republicans took over Congress, there were 1,318 earmarks, for a total of $7.8 billion. Yet in 2006, the last year Republicans were in charge of Congress before getting ousted, there were 9,963 earmarks totaling $29 billion. Education, health care, transportation, and numerous other programs grew enormously during that same time, most without any serious consideration of the enumerated powers of Congress.[21]

• *Medicare Part D:* While putting the federal government in the pharmacy business, Medicare Part D just expanded a broken program further and increased unfunded liabilities by $17 trillion.[22] Senate Republicans supported the measure 42–9, while House Republicans supported it 204–25.[23]

• *Immigration:* Washington Republicans decided it was necessary to pass Comprehensive Immigration Reform, which was largely an effort to avoid taking on the core federal responsibility of enforcing our nation's borders. With a 55-strong majority in 2006, Republicans chose to spend valuable political capital and time pushing a bill that would garner only 23 Republican votes on final passage (more Democrats voted for it than Republicans).

Meanwhile, the border remained open and Republicans lost the majority in November of that year.

• *Bailouts:* Republicans joined hand in hand with Democrats under a sky-is-falling mentality, to pass TARP (the big bailout), auto industry bailouts, and Fannie and Freddie bailouts — generally committing more than a trillion dollars while turning the American economy on its head. On TARP, Senate Republicans voted in favor 33–15, House Republicans a slightly more respectable 91–108.[24]

This, of course, doesn't touch the significant number of unprincipled votes I have left uncovered, such as Republican support for steel tariffs; for the unconstitutional McCain-Feingold restriction on free speech; for creation of the massive new Department of Homeland Security; for the Sarbanes-Oxley regulatory reform, which is driving business overseas; and for regulation of carbon dioxide.

The Political Winds of Change Are Blowing

By spending like drunkards and abandoning principle, Republicans went from a massive majority in 2004 to a massive minority in just four years. Meanwhile, many establishment Republicans in Washington want to blame their losses on the war in Iraq. I simply do not believe that is true. While Americans rightly have a watchful eye on the commitment of our courageous soldiers to the Middle East, and while many Americans still want to hear a clear articulation of our mission there, most Americans realize the need to combat terror on their turf, not ours.

The real reason for our loss of the majority was not an unpopular war, but a compromising of our principles as a party when it came to limited government and limited spending. That used to be our trump card—the one issue we could fall back on when all else was going wrong in a political context. But it was gone by 2006, and—along with uncertainty about the war and scandals that showed our members of Congress are all too human—it meant our brand was in shambles. I even recall one survey after that election that showed Democrats were more trusted on taxes and spending than Republicans, and I simply couldn't remember the last time that was the case.

The good news is that the people are taking action. The Tea Party movement began in earnest as the result of boiling frustration among Americans, triggered by the dramatic expansion of government into their private affairs through bailouts and so-called stimulus plans. Hundreds of thousands of people around the country—ordinary folks—gathered at Tea Parties and organized protests and marches in towns across America and in Washington. While most Democrats have been dismissive of the Tea Parties—just witness the vulgar terminology used by MSNBC pundits whose sophomoric zealotry has no match on modern-day cable news—the Republican Party has been a hotbed of political activity in primaries, where Tea Party activists and other frustrated Americans are having a real impact.

There is a movement afoot to send to Washington people who represent the people, instead of themselves or the political establishment. But happily, there is recognition that the Republican Party is the place where the real debate is happening—and the result has been the nomination of nonestablishment candidates in states across the country: notably, U.S. Senate candidates Marco Rubio in Florida over incumbent moderate governor Charlie Crist, Rand Paul over the preferred establishment candidate Trey Grayson in Kentucky, Joe Miller over incumbent moderate Lisa Murkowski in Alaska, and perhaps most interesting was the takedown of longtime Republican Senator Bob Bennett in the Utah primary. You see, Utah is a very conservative state—and Bob Bennett had teamed up with liberal Democrat Ron Wyden to put together a liberal Washington-type health care plan only slightly different from Obamacare, and the people of Utah sent a message that this was not acceptable.

What is astonishing, however, is that a few establishment Republicans in Washington still do not seem to get it. Consider for example that in the face of the efforts by the American people to demand change through the Tea Party movement, Senator Lindsey Graham (R-SC) said, "the Tea Party movement will die out,"[25] and worse, according to the congressional newspaper *The Hill*, Senator Bob Bennett (R-UT) "suggested the movement simply thrives off of voter anger and does not act rationally."[26] This is the same Senator Graham who supported amnesty for illegal immigrants, voted for Justices Sotomayor and Kagan, and negotiates with Democrats on costly environmental regulations, immigration, and numerous other measures. But the prize goes to none other than former Republican leader Trent Lott, who said, "As soon as [the rabble-rousers] get here, we need to co-opt them."[27] I am proud that I was the first governor to call for Lott to step down as majority leader for his sentimental fawning over the good ole days back in 2002.

Given all this, is it really *hard to believe* that Americans are jaded about Congress? Simple observation or a quick look at most any recent favorability poll of Americans demonstrates the total lack of respect for federal politicians on both sides of the aisle. Indeed, according to Gallup, as of June 2010 only 1 in 5 Americans approved of the job Congress is doing, up from 16 percent in March.[28] According to the Rasmussen Reports, in July 2010, 87 percent of Americans gave Congress either a poor or a fair rating.[29] But Republicans aren't loved much either, as the same poll showed that a full 72 percent of Republican voters believe "GOP members of Congress have lost touch" with the party base.[30] Most tellingly, some 78 percent of respondents believe that "most members of Congress are more interested in helping their own careers than in helping people."[31] And institutionally, respect for Congress has reached rock bottom — only 11 percent of Americans rate highly their confidence in Congress as of July 2010.[32]

The much anticipated Republican gains in 2010 should not breed cockiness in GOP leaders. The change sought by the American people is not simply political change, but a change from the status quo — a change from the way things have been working (or not working) in Washington for far too long; a change that will tilt the balance of power away from Washington and to the states and the people. And as long as Republicans are willing to accept the status quo in Washington and choose the establishment over the people, then the political winds will continue to bat the power of Congress back and forth like a Ping-Pong ball rather than creating a long-term conservative Republican majority. If Republicans don't get it right this time, I am afraid we will go the way of the Whigs, because the American people are looking for leaders who will stand athwart history, and fight.

9

States Do the Work of the People

If the States look with apathy on this silent descent of their government into the gulf [of consolidation] which is to swallow all, we have only to weep over the human character formed uncontrollable but by a rod of iron, and the blasphemers of man as incapable of self-government become his true historians.

— THOMAS JEFFERSON, LETTER TO CHARLES HAMMOND, 1821[1]

AT APPROXIMATELY 8:30 A.M. on the morning of August 31, 2005, I received a phone call from Governor Kathleen Blanco of Louisiana. Her state was in the midst of responding to the destruction left in the wake of Hurricane Katrina and the failure of the levees that protect low-lying New Orleans. The sheer scale of the devastation and the loss of life was unimaginable but yet so very real as it unfolded before our eyes. In the days following the hurricane, more than 80 percent of the city was flooded.[2] Shelters for survivors were over capacity. At the main shelter set up at the Superdome in New Orleans, "the air conditioning failed, the water pressure dropped, and the turf field, plastic seats, and concrete ramps and corridors were overflowing with hungry, dehydrated, and exhausted evacuees."[3]

In the face of these conditions, Governor Blanco asked me if Texas would consider helping the people of Louisiana by giving shelter to evacuees who were homeless and in need. There was never a question in my mind and, to be honest, our decision to offer support had already been made. Texans had been preparing in the days following the hurricane's landfall on August 29 to offer help if it was needed.

Our state's emergency management team, a division within the Department of Public Safety, was working with local officials across Texas to be ready for possible evacuees. Judge Robert Eckels was in charge of the Citizen Corps in Harris County, Texas, a program launched by President Bush in the aftermath of 9/11, to be set up by local citizens to respond to area emergencies, and he coordinated with state, federal, and Louisiana officials. In fact, a 6:00 a.m. conference phone call that took place before I even spoke with Governor Blanco had already set the wheels in motion to receive some 23,000 refugees if requested.[4] The schedule was cleared for the Astrodome through December, and the Federal Emergency Management Agency (FEMA) was preparing some 475 buses for the convoy from New Orleans to Houston.[5]

At 10:30 a.m. that morning, the American Red Cross asked how many volunteers in Harris County were available to prepare the Astrodome. A message was sent to the Harris County Citizen Corps e-mail list, "announcing that New Orleans evacuees were on their way to Houston, and that Harris County 'must build a city ready to receive them.'"[6] The response was overwhelming — over 1,000 responses per hour resulting in over 2,800 new members and 38 new organizations.[7] According to the Citizen Corps, "In the first 24 hours, the Harris County Citizen Corps processed over 8,000 volunteers to assist the ARC in its activities. Over the course of the county's operations, volunteer coordinators averaged 3,500 spontaneous volunteers processed each day."[8]

On September 1, I officially declared a state of emergency for the people of Texas, which triggered a host of state laws we have in place, as well as cooperative agreements under federal law, to make crisis management easier — such as temporary access to prescription medicine without a prescription, easier quarantine procedures, and temporary physician licenses.[9] In addition, to try to minimize the disruption to the lives of the people who had lost so much, we coordinated among the public schools in the area to take in some 5,485 New Orleans children.[10] Later that day, it became clear to us that Louisiana needed more help — and that we needed to prepare for an additional 50,000 folks from New Orleans.[11]

We immediately set the wheels in motion to prepare Dallas and San Antonio to receive an additional 25,000 evacuees each, using the Reunion Arena and the old Kelly Air Force Base as initial shelters. We also began to prepare other cities in the state, and I ordered the Texas Department of Housing and Community Affairs to ready some 7,000 low-income housing units for use.[12] Tens of thousands of additional refugees were staying in hotels and in the homes of Texans who had opened their doors. In the end, we believe, Texas absorbed more than 200,000 of our Louisiana neighbors — opening up our schools, our state parks, our hospitals and clinics, as long as needed. We even shared our athletic facilities, so that Tulane University and the New Orleans Saints (who would go on to win the Super Bowl in 2010) could have a home to play football.

This experience taught me a lot about people. With the possible exception of spending time with our valiant men and women in uniform, I have never been more proud to be a Texan than when I watched how quickly and passionately our people responded to the basic human needs of our neighbors. But I shouldn't be surprised. That is what we do. That is how good people react to tragedy and people in need. You don't sit around and point fingers and ask who is going to do something, you just do it. In the end, for all the criticisms of how things transpired in the wake of Hurricane Katrina, what I saw in Texas made me proud.

I recall that on the night of my call with Governor Blanco, during a brief appearance with Chris Matthews on MSNBC, he asked me, "Where's Texas getting the money for this?" I responded, "Well, you know, we will find the dollars. The fact of the matter is...by the grace of God, this could have been Houston, Texas, that we were talking about today, instead of New Orleans. And our neighbors are in need and we will find the dollars to make it work." That's what I believed then, and that's how we'd approach a similar situation again.

In the aftermath of Katrina, it goes without saying that the federal government had numerous roles, from organizing transportation to having set up the Citizens Corps network that helped us organize from the ground up in the first place. Some of it worked, some of it didn't. Of course, the federal government should have a role in dealing with a massive disaster that affected such a large part of the nation. My frustration mounts in particular, however, when the federal government impedes crucial work. We can fight about money tomorrow. But today, when we need action, get out of the way.

After Katrina, we faced numerous challenges as the federal government bureaucracy dragged its feet. As tens of thousands of people poured into our state, FEMA was not helping us find housing. Worse, though, they were prohibiting us from working with other states to spread folks out, which would have been better for everyone involved. We were working on an airlift, which was then blocked by the federal government. Utah governor Jon Huntsman offered to divert a military transport plane and send buses, even risking not getting federal reimbursement, but he was stalled by FEMA and the Defense Department. Other states, such as West Virginia, were rejected by FEMA because they were "too far away."[13]

And months following the Katrina disaster, when there was time to absorb the lessons of bureaucratic failings at all government levels, what was the federal government's response? They want to federalize more of the disaster response. I think former governor Jeb Bush of Florida, who knows a lot about hurricane response, summed up my thoughts well when he said, "I can say with certainty that federalizing emergency response to catastrophic events would be a disaster as bad as Hurricane Katrina. The current system works when everyone understands, accepts, and is willing to fulfill their responsibilities.... The bottom-up approach yields the best results."[14]

Here, the people of Houston, and ultimately throughout Texas, stepped up to the plate. They did the vast majority of the work and the organization, getting together the cots, blankets, pillows, security, food, medicine, water, and all the basic necessities of life. They enrolled children in schools and organized a network of people to open their homes. They did so because it was the right thing to do. Of course, it didn't come free from difficulties. There were plenty of speed bumps and bickering, and I can tell you that tempers flared.

But they got the job done. And it is through states that the American people get the job done every day, often in spite of a deeply flawed bureaucratic federal government. States sometimes must pick up the ball that has been dropped by the federal government—and, shockingly, must fight a federal government that tells them they can't do it. The states offer the American people one of the only means for pushing back on a federal government that is overstepping its bounds more and more every day.

We saw similar problems in the aftermath of the recent oil spill in the Gulf of Mexico. Governor Jindal faced a dilemma. Oil was approaching his state and threatening sensitive environmental areas, wildlife habitats, and the important economy built upon a vibrant, healthy coastline. The governor wanted to take action to protect his state and the people who live there. For example, he wanted to build a barrier off the coast to slow down the progress of the oil—and he was told "no" by the Army Corp of Engineers. He wanted to move sixteen vacuum barges into operation but was, again, told "no," without any particular reason.[15] While these skimmers ultimately were put into operation,[16] the governor repeatedly expressed frustration with federal bureaucratic red tape when it came to getting them into place and taking other action he felt appropriate.[17]

Maybe Governor Jindal was right. Or maybe he was wrong with respect to any of these decisions. I don't much care. Because as the guy on the ground trying to protect the people of his state, I tend to defer to Jindal's judgment and his level of commitment to solving the problem in the first place. It is his home, after all.

States Do the Work of the People

State and local governments, by being closest to the people, bring out the best of both self- and representative government. When local government calls the shots, the people making decisions know how lives are affected on the ground, and leave maximum room for people to improvise and innovate without having to ask permission. There will be mistakes, there will be flaws. But I believe that in the end mistakes are minimized and less arbitrary when the person facing the actual problem firsthand is the person making the decision—not some FEMA employee or bureaucrat at the Department of Defense thousands of miles away.

And we see this every day in our lives. Most of the things you use every day are, thankfully, still provided by the private sector. Buying a car, getting gas, buying groceries, going out to eat at a restaurant, getting supplies at a hardware store, buying clothes, getting a computer or most anything you need every single day. But for those things that do require government, the things that most affect you every day are run by local or state governments. Local schools, police, sheriffs, firefighters, roads, public utilities such as water, and all of the other things that affect your life on a day-to-day basis are taken care of by your neighbors, your friends, members of your family, or fellow churchgoers. You know them, or if you don't, at least they live among you in your community or are just down the road in the state capital.

The American people often don't know how many good things are going on in their states because of the dominance of the national news and events today. In the 24-hour news cycle, many of the stories we hear about have to do with the President, the Congress, what states supposedly are doing wrong (think Arizona and its immigration law), what federal legislation we "must" have, and how much money "must" be spent.

Take a look at Texas. Most people — even Texans — have no idea that Texas established water and air pollution programs before Congress passed federal clean water and air legislation.[18] Most people don't know that Texas produces the most wind power and has the largest wind farm of any state in the nation.[19] Most people don't know that Texas is leading the nation with a successful effort to deregulate electricity that has helped with the growth of alternative "green" energies as well as provided choice for consumers. As one article put it:

> The past ten years have brought improved reliability to Texas' growing energy demands. The old regulated system never

could have kept up. Because of deregulation, there are more generation developments and greener innovations that make power more efficiently. There is now more reliability in power transmission with efficiency cutting both waste and energy cost in Texas. And finally, market competition has stimulated generators and retailers to cut their costs to deliver better service at a lower price to consumers.... That's why all the other states are following Texas.[20]

Of course most people don't know that, because all we are ever taught is that the federal government is the only one that "cares" about the environment. The federal government's view of Texans suggests that we'd prefer to run around destroying the parks in which we like to hike, the water we drink, the air we breathe, and otherwise ruin the great landscape God has given us. Hardly. Texas has a great track record of protecting the environment, and I am proud of it. As I discussed earlier, our regulatory process actually achieves results and the air quality in Texas has improved more dramatically than in many other states under the federal government's we-know-best policies.

Responsible State and Local Governments Give Value to the Taxpayer

If you consider the impact of state and local governments on your life and their relative value provided as compared with that provided by the federal government, it sure seems to me that the size and scope is backwards.

In 2007, the average Texan paid $1,691 in state tax, $1,750 in local tax, and a whopping $8,916 in federal tax. Let's go ahead and account for defense spending, which most of us agree is important and constitutionally required of the federal government. About 25 percent of the budget is focused on security (which includes things beyond core defense, such as parts of homeland security). So, discounting for our national security, the average Texan paid about $6,687 for other federal spending, right at about *twice* what he spent for state and local services combined.

Keep in mind that since 2007, federal spending has literally exploded by about $1 trillion, so the relative tax burden we face may well become far more lopsided. Plus, what we pay in federal taxes today doesn't come close to covering what we spend, because the federal government has borrowed trillions of dollars — banknotes that will eventually come due to the taxpayer, with interest. The President's Fiscal Commission, cochaired by Democrat Erskine Bowles and former senator Alan Simpson, is hinting that there will be significant tax hikes on the table.[21] They are musing about a 3 to 1 spending-cut-to-tax-increase ratio to solve the fiscal crisis we face. Given what we know about the size of the unfunded liabilities for entitlements ($108 trillion), and the lack of political courage to deal with that problem, what does your common sense tell you? You will get massively higher taxes in the form of a value-added tax (VAT), higher income taxes, or both; you will see cuts in military spending and other proper federal concerns — and you will get zero fiscal responsibility from Washington.

It's no wonder Americans are so angry. It's not that there isn't some value from that nondefense spending, and it's not that Americans are not comfortable with some of it. It's just that Washington is so darned irresponsible with our money and it defies common sense to send vastly more resources there than you give to the governments that actually provide you some degree of service. Moreover, let's look at the extent of responsibility of those levels of government. Texas spent (in 2009) $1,729 per capita, which is, not surprisingly, very close to the level of tax collected.

On the other hand, the federal government spent (in 2009) approximately $19,840 per capita, which is almost twice the amount of tax collected. In Texas, per capita debt is approximately $520, while federal per capita debt is approximately $42,600. Expressed as a percent of tax collections, Texas could retire its debt by dedicating less than four months of taxes to debt retirement. To retire the federal debt would require Washington to dedicate 100 percent of its tax collections for almost five years. Now, not every state is as responsible as Texas. California, for example, is struggling to get its budget balanced. But, even it, unlike Washington, is trying to make the hard choices to do so.

Like at least 45 of our sister states, Texas faces budget challenges as revenues decline in the current economic climate.[22] The strong Texas economy is not immune to the international slowdown. But in the face of this reality, Texans are buckling down and figuring out what to do about it. Unlike Washington, we also have a rainy-day fund of just over $8 billion. We don't want to tap it unless we must, so just like we did in 2003, we are already working to cut spending to close the gap before we get to our next legislative session. It's hard work, it's challenging, but it's the right thing to do. And, I might add, it's what our families do when they hit tough times. Quite frankly, most U.S. workers can't walk into the boss's office and demand a raise simply because their income doesn't meet their spending obligations. Instead, they find items to cut to survive a rough patch. Government seems to think it can demand a raise whenever it likes — in fact, thinks it is entitled to one — justifying tax hikes on the worthiness of the programs it wants to fund. If only liberals thought about the people paying the taxes as much as it does those receiving subsidized services.

Texas is not the only state that has managed to get its budget in good shape. In 2009, the Commonwealth of Virginia elected Governor Bob McDonnell, who had inherited a deficit of $1.8 billion, projected to reach $4.2 billion over 2011 and 2012. As the governor said, they did it by "cutting spending, reducing our budget estimates to a realistic amount, and making sure that we're doing what American families and businesses do, and that is don't spend more than you take in. It's a pretty simple formula."[23] In just one year, the governor turned that deficit into a $220 million surplus. And newly elected Republican governor Chris Christie is turning heads in tax-strapped New Jersey by working through the closure of an $11 billion budget gap in 2010.[24] As noted in the *Economist,* he has "taken on a notoriously cranky legislature and has stared down the powerful teachers' union. He has even refused to reappoint a judge to New Jersey's activist Supreme Court." This is how we get things done in states with a little courage and wherewithal.[25]

State and local governments are not perfect. We all have lots of waste we can end, lots of bureaucratic red tape we need to streamline ourselves, and we have laws that could be improved to maximize freedom. But the value proposition offered by state and local governments as compared with the federal government is, in fact, incomparable. Imagine how strong we could be if the federal government didn't interfere with us and if we didn't often have to do its job.

States Sometimes Must Fill the Federal Void

When the federal government fails to take care of its core responsibilities in its quixotic quest to solve the problems of the world, sometimes it's impossible for states to help. For example, national defense is a function left to the federal government, and states can't step in when Washington drops the ball on something like missile defense. But occasionally, there are areas in which states can take action.

In the face of the federal government's failure to secure our nation's borders from illegal entry, border states face a very real problem each and every day. In response, in early 2010 Arizona passed a law that suddenly became the center of a firestorm of controversy. It was designed to require state and local law enforcement officers to do what they were empowered to do, and that is to check the immigration status of someone already engaged in a lawful stop, when the officers reasonably suspect him or her of being here illegally. The law targeted primarily so-called sanctuary cities — to make sure that no local mayors, sheriffs, or other leaders were able to ignore enforcement of immigration laws.

Now, the national controversy has been largely disingenuous — based on misinformation and fearmongering. Governor Brewer and the Arizona legislature took a modest step to fill the breach caused by the failure of the federal government — and are completely within their rights to do so. And in fact, large numbers of illegals apprehended away from the borders — that is, once living in our communities — are regularly apprehended or discovered by local law enforcement. They're picked up on some local crime, from a DUI or parking ticket to domestic abuse or something else. State and local law enforcement cooperates with the Department of Homeland Security and together they decide what steps to take. All Arizona is doing is telling its law enforcement not to turn a blind eye. That's the purpose. I do have some concerns with the law, and I don't believe it is necessarily the right approach for Texas, in part because of the new cause of action it provides against law enforcement. Having battled trial lawyers for decades, I am concerned about opening up the courthouse doors to additional lawsuits. But I strongly support the right of the citizens of Arizona, Texas, or any other state to pass laws to protect themselves. In fact, we joined in federal court with eight other states to help defend Arizona against the Obama administration's lawsuit.

The national controversy became surreal as President Obama and Attorney General Eric Holder embarked on an arrogant and misguided effort to sue Arizona in court. I can tell you that as a governor, I found that insulting and almost unbelievable, even for this administration. But the fight is all politics. It's not about the actual law. The only evidence you need is that the attorney general was publicly stating that the law might be unconstitutional and might cause racial profiling and that he was considering whether he would challenge it in court—*all while having never actually read the bill*.[26]

As this book went to print, a Clinton-appointed federal judge issued an injunction against parts of the Arizona law. In what can only be described as a blatant example of judicial activism, the judge claimed that "requiring Arizona law enforcement officials and agencies to determine the immigration status of every person who is arrested burdens lawfully-present aliens because their liberty will be restricted while their status is checked. Even though Arizona's interests may be consistent with those of the federal government, it is not in the public interest for Arizona to enforce pre-empted laws."[27] The judge essentially made this policy up out of thin air and in the process spit in the face of federalism and the right of the people to govern themselves.

Pushing Back on Washington

Couple the kind of arrogance exhibited above by the federal government with its incompetence and unconstitutional forays into the sphere of the states, and the people are forcing those states to push back. We are seeing this phenomenon play out in multiple ways and contexts and, not surprisingly, Texans are right in the middle of it.

Important less for its practical effect than for the message it sends, a number of states have introduced resolutions reaffirming their belief in and support of the Tenth Amendment to the Constitution. I was proud to support the introduction of such a resolution by State Representative Brandon Creighton in 2009 when I said, "I believe that our federal government has become oppressive in its size, its intrusion into the lives of our citizens, and its interference with the affairs of our state.... That is why I am here today to express my unwavering support for efforts all across our country to reaffirm states' rights affirmed by the Tenth Amendment to the U.S. Constitution."[28]

More important, however, has been the immediate response by states to the passage of nationalized health care —both legislatively and in court. Some 37 states have introduced measures designed to protect citizens from the federal law that the states believe is unconstitutional,[29] and court action is well under way—with two primary cases moving forward. First is litigation being brought by Attorney General Ken Cuccinelli on behalf of the Commonwealth of Virginia, which is proceeding with its own challenge to the federal health care law because of a unique provision in its state law. Meanwhile, Florida is leading a multistate challenge that also includes Texas, South Carolina, Nebraska, Utah, Louisiana, Alabama, Colorado, Michigan, Pennsylvania, Washington, Idaho, and South Dakota.[30] There are any number of arguments to make, but the core issue generally revolves around whether the federal government can mandate that private citizens must go out and buy health care insurance in the private market. Of course the Constitution does not provide that authority, but the question remains nonetheless whether the courts will see it that way.

Take a look also at state involvement in our individual right to keep and bear arms. At least 40 states have laws on the books allowing their citizens to carry a weapon in some form or another, and many of those have reciprocity agreements with other states.[31] And there has been a flurry of activity in recent years to continue to improve state laws in this area. But recently a number of states have also begun pushing back against what they perceive as the overreach of federal law against their citizens through the Commerce Clause. For example, as I discussed earlier, there are numerous federal gun laws that reach down into areas traditionally left to the states. Montana and Tennessee, for example, are getting tired of that, so they passed laws to protect from federal reach firearms that are manufactured and sold entirely within the state. Virginia is considering a similar measure.[32]

But perhaps most interesting is a movement I disagree with, while appreciating the desire of Californians to decide for themselves — and this is the issue of marijuana consumption. A few years ago, Californians legalized the limited medicinal use of marijuana, but the Supreme Court struck this law down in *Gonzales v. Raich,* claiming that the federal government has the power to regulate activity that would have a substantial effect on interstate commerce.[33] Now, I am not sure the people of Texas would want to go down this road, but it sure seems to me that Justice Thomas got this one right when he said in dissent:

> The majority prevents States like California from devising drug policies that they have concluded provide much-needed respite to the seriously ill.... The majority's rush to embrace federal power "is especially unfortunate given the importance of showing respect for the sovereign States that comprise our Federal Union." United States v. Oakland Cannabis Buyers' Cooperative, 532 U.S. 483, 502 (2001) (Stevens, J., concurring in judgment). Our federalist system, properly understood, allows California and a growing number of other States to decide for themselves how to safeguard the

health and welfare of their citizens. I would affirm the judgment of the Court of Appeals. I respectfully dissent.[34]

The natural question that this kind of conflict between federal and state goals raises is, How, then, do the laws get enforced? The Supreme Court made crystal clear in *United States v. Printz,* a case involving the enforcement of temporary provisions of the Brady Handgun Violence Prevention Act, that the federal government cannot commandeer state authorities to carry out federal law.[35] Now, keeping in mind that in 2008, less than 1 percent of the 847,000 marijuana-related arrests were carried out by federal law enforcement, it sure seems unlikely that there could be adequate resources at the federal level to actually tell Californians how to live their lives.[36] In other words, Californians may well be telling the federal government to "bring it on," we'll handle this how we want to handle it. Why, then, is it so controversial when a Texas governor raises questions about other issues, such as nationalized health care, energy, the environment, or federal mandates regarding education?

Consider efforts in Congress to interfere with the rights of states to regulate oil and gas exploration. In a classic overreaction to a tragic environmental disaster that occurred in a federal lease area, Congress felt the need to consider taking increased regulatory power over areas traditionally left to the states. In a July 2010 letter to the Texas congressional delegation, numerous Texas state leaders joined me in calling for rejection of such a misguided expansion of federal power in direct contradiction to the Tenth Amendment and for the federal government to focus on those things it can control — such as the failure of federal laws and regulations that led to the Deepwater Horizon disaster in the first place.[37]

A number of states are also telling the federal government that they are sick and tired of having tax dollars taken from their citizens, only to be held over their head in the form of bribery or coercion to fall in line with yet another federal requirement. I was heavily criticized by the press and the Democrats—though funnily by not all that many taxpayers—when in 2009 I made the decision that Texas should turn down $556 million of the federal "stimulus" money. The problem was that the money, which the federal government had designated for the unemployed, came with unprecedented changes to our state rules that would have affected eligibility for unemployment. Worse, Texas businesses would have been left paying additional costs once the federal money was no longer available. It would have been irresponsible to take the money.

I was faced with a similar choice, where you are damned if you do and damned if you don't, again in 2010 when it came to additional education funding. Up to $700 million in additional federal stimulus money was this time being offered to states through the Department of Education's $5 billion Race to the Top (RTTT) program. I turned down the money because under the program we would have been required to adopt national standards without knowing what they would be and doing so would have further inserted Washington into the Texas classroom. And more than that, it would have cost us some $3 billion to change all our textbooks and materials to comply with the Washington standards.

Ultimately, the decision was easy for two reasons. First, the Texas school system is performing well, with leading standards, strong accountability, a strong college preparatory curriculum, and innovative charter schools. Second, the money we turned down was about $75 per student and only enough to pay for the operation of Texas public schools for about two days.[38] It is frustrating when we are put in this position of turning down what is, in effect, our own money, but at some point we have to start telling Washington that we've had enough of the strings they attach and we're not just going to blindly accept what's offered. Texas was not the only state to choose not to compete for the money, but President Obama and other Washington Democrats have placed a target on the backs of Texas leaders nonetheless.

In fact, later in 2010, House Democrats inserted into a war supplemental bill a $10 billion education component that had language targeting Texas specifically. The provision would make money available to certain Texas school districts only if I certified that it would not be used to "replace" state money — even though I cannot make such a certification without violating the Texas Constitution. This is the merry-go-round of federal funding with strings. It seems at times that our federal officials live in an *Alice in Wonderland* type of world, where up is down.

I believe that the American people are eminently capable of taking care of themselves. I believe we see this each and every day with the work being carried out by the people at the state and local level. If the federal government continues to step beyond its enumerated powers and continues to tell the American people how to live their lives, states will continue to push back. There is no getting around that. Whether it is education, health care, guns, immigration, marijuana, school prayer, or any issue that resonates with the people at a very personal level, they will not just sit back and say, "Thank you, sir, may I have another?" each time the federal government slaps them upside the head with a mandate from on high or another failure to do its job. That is not how the American people think. The federal goverment must respect the Constitution so we once again can live in the freedom it protects.

10

Retaking the Reins of Government: Freedom and Federalism for the Future

> *As the patriots of seventy-six did to the support of the*
> *Declaration of Independence, so to the support of the*
> *Constitution and Laws, let every American pledge his*
> *life, his property, and his sacred honor.*
>
> — ABRAHAM LINCOLN, JANUARY 27, 1838[1]

IN JUST FIFTEEN YEARS, our nation will be preparing to celebrate its 250th birthday. It is notable that we commemorate as our birthday July 4, 1776, the date we associate with our declaration of independence. It was at that moment, of course, that America's founding generation told the world that they were fed up with a faraway government telling them how to live their lives, and they risked everything they had—indeed, they "pledged their lives, their fortunes and their sacred honour"—as they joined together in the fight to be free.

That was the spirit of 1776.

I want to call for the awakening of that independent spirit on which the United States was founded. Let us work together to restore our founding principles, but also to retake the reins of government and chart a path forward for a new age of liberty in America. As we approach this historic milestone in 2026, we owe our great nation — and all those patriots who came before us who have toiled, struggled, bled, and even died to protect her — the greatest birthday present we can give. We need to fulfill a promise: that we will pass down to the next generation a stronger and freer America, so that they may not be born into debt, or into servitude to a powerful government every bit as tyrannical as a monarchy. As Jefferson said: "When all government, domestic and foreign, in little as in great things, shall be drawn to Washington as the center of all power, it will render powerless the checks provided of one government on another and will become as venal and oppressive as the government from which we separated."[2]

It is our duty to ensure that the next generation shall inherit their birthright as Americans — the right to live free, according to the dictates of their own conscience and their willingness to wake up every day to make the most of their God-given opportunity.

We can do this. The American people do great things every day. We are a hardworking, God-fearing people who love to help our neighbors. There is nothing we have not been able to accomplish in the past and there is nothing we cannot accomplish in the future if we will promote liberty, personal responsibility, and limited government over the false promise of government-provided comfort in this imperfect world. We are better than that. Indeed, we have defined for the world what being better than that truly means and we cannot allow succeeding generations of Americans to miss out on what it was like to live free. We cannot allow an all-powerful federal government to dictate how we live, and to strip from the world its last, best hope.

Freedom and Federalism for the Future

In 2026, I picture an America ascendant. I see a nation filled with diverse people bound together by a commitment to liberty and a devotion to working hard to give to their children a better life than their parents gave them. I see a great nation, where day by day, more and more people here and around the world have the clothes, food, housing, medicine, and other necessities of life because of the hard work, goodwill, and love for freedom of the American people—not the tired, ineffective, interfering "work" of some "benevolent" bureaucrat in Washington. I see a nation that is being run by the people at the level of government closest to them, flourishing amid a rebirth of federalism and local control.

As a result, I see a nation where deficits are a thing of the past and mounting debt is no longer the millstone around the neck of our children's children that it is today. I see a federal budget that is balanced and a people who live according to their means rather than the whims of an irresponsible and deceitful federal government. I see a federal government that no longer wastes the people's money, but uses it efficiently to perform only the basic tasks assigned to it. And I see a Congress that no longer doles out pork in a corrupt effort to buy votes back home, but actually develops an appropriations process that earns the trust of the American people.

I see a federal government that focuses on the few things for which it is empowered and well suited—such as national defense, border enforcement, and foreign commerce—and does them well. I see a Congress that meets less often and for less time, and when it does meet actually debates the difficult issues of the day rather than preening for cameras. I see a Congress that actually reads the bills it passes, and that passes shorter, understandable bills rather than longer, incomprehensible ones. For, as James Madison said in the *Federalist Papers* over 200 years ago, "It will be of little avail to the people that the laws are made by men of their own choice, if the laws be so voluminous that they cannot be read, or so incoherent that they cannot be understood."[3]

I see a nation where the people and their own doctors get to decide how to care for their families. I see individuals who own their own health insurance policies and that those policies are not controlled by employers, can account for preexisting conditions, and have affordable prices driven down by robust competition. I see states that have allowed for greater competition across their borders for insurance companies. I see doctors who are not afraid to go into the health field because trial lawyers are no longer allowed to hold them hostage to runaway, abusive lawsuits. And I see millions of lives continuing to be saved by our nation's many advancements in medicine.

I see an entitlement system that has been totally and honestly revamped—where $106 trillion in unfunded liabilities are met with innovation, decentralization, and real solutions rather than false promises. There will be a retirement safety net that is no longer set up like an illegal Ponzi scheme, but rather will allow individuals to own and control their own retirement. There will be a health care safety net that is not built on the promise of what government can provide for the people, but on what individuals can accomplish together over our lifetime through work, savings, charity—and by spreading risk out through insurance policies.

I see a people who can pray in their schools as they wish, and towns across America that can publicly celebrate Christmas, Hanukkah, or nothing at all. I see great organizations such as the Boy Scouts, who are free to assemble as they wish and according to their own beliefs and ideals. I see a country that allows the people, and not the courts, to define marriage according to their wishes and morals. And I see a world in which the unborn are allowed a chance at life, unfettered by an activist court telling them what is right and what is wrong.

I see an education system that is the envy of the world, controlled by parents and the people according to the beliefs of the communities in which they live. I see an energetic mix of public, charter, and private schools delivering options so that people can choose what is best for their children, rather then getting stuck because a too powerful teachers' union or government bureaucrat tells them how they must learn. The result is an important balance of academic excellence, local values, and a firm understanding of our nation's core founding principles—all of which will carry our nation forward with new generations of American achievement.

I see an America that has the strongest economy in the world—where the innovation and hard work of the American people create still more opportunities, jobs, and wealth for generations of Americans and the rest of the world. I see a nation that is not cowering to the prospect of a united Europe or an ever-growing China and India, but rather welcomes those markets and many others as opportunities for the entrepreneurial and industrious spirit of the American people. I see a world where free trade opens up more doors and where people embrace trade's benefit to both America and the rest of the world.

I see an America that has the strongest national defense in the world, by an insurmountable order of magnitude. I see defense technology that is miles beyond our allies or adversaries, and servicemen and women who are better trained and equipped than anyone. I see a functional missile defense system protecting us and our allies, and I see modernized fleets of ships and aircraft that are unsurpassed in their ability to overwhelm the enemy. I see a world where America promotes peace through the strength of her forces, which continue to be used to protect freedom rather than in conquest.

I see an America—led by the states and the people who live there—that has clean air, clean water, ample green space, and an environment filled with abundant wildlife. I also see an America with abundant energy, a generous mix of wind, solar, and hydro-electric power; fossil fuels; and many other resources of which we are blessed with large quantities. There is no reason we cannot lead the world in developing clean energy while continuing to fuel our economy with the energy it needs to create wealth, jobs, and opportunity.

I see a nation where people are not judged by the color of their skin—as they are today behind the facade of ending discrimination. I see a world where race-based thinking is relegated to the bigot in the corner and not embraced by our nation's laws in the form of affirmative action, flawed incarnations of the Voting Rights Act, or ideas like a race-based Native Hawaiian government—the mind-boggling effort of some in Congress to create a separate government for those with a drop of native Hawaiian blood (just Google it—it's unbelievable).

I see a world where America continues to open its arms to the world so that more people may have a chance at the American dream. And I see a nation that enforces its borders so that the rule of law may be respected, so that the nation will not be burdened by an onslaught of people living in the shadows, and so that the very people who try to come here will not be forced to risk their lives while doing so only to run and hide in an endless revolving door that is neither good for them nor for our nation.

Ultimately, I see a world where all things that can be done by the individual are done by him and no one else. I see a world where all things that cannot be done by the individual are first facilitated by families, friends, colleagues, and those close to him.

I see a world where communities and local government step in to fill the breach, and where states step in only when necessary. But most of all, I see a world where the federal government involves itself as the last resort, and only according to its constitutionally prescribed powers.

That is the world I want to live in—a world where people are free and government is minimized, and as a result we live in prosperity according to our own hard work and responsibility, backstopped by family, friends, private charity, insurance, and, when necessary and appropriate, state and local government. That, of course, was the world envisioned by our Founders. As the Father of the Constitution, James Madison, said, "The government of the United States is a definite government, confined to specified objects. It is not like the state governments, whose powers are more general. Charity is no part of the legislative duty of the government."[4] That is the purpose of our "dual sovereign" structure in which federalism guarantees that decision-making can and will occur closest to the people and that the powers in Washington were to be specifically enumerated and confined. This is the world we must restore.

Taking Back America

So, can we do this? The cynics will say it is impossible—that this is too much to ask for and that we should just take whatever we can get from Washington. Nonsense.

We are Americans. Of course we can have the world we want to live in. The federal government is not some magical oracle on high from which all knowledge and truth comes. Quite the opposite, actually. Our government is "of the people, by the people and for the people," as Abraham Lincoln so eloquently stated in the Gettysburg Address. This is *our* government. We get to decide,

up to turn down money from Washington — be it the misguided use of stimulus money for unemployment insurance or for the additional Race to the Top educations funds, all coming with federal strings and requirements — I was excoriated in the press and by my Democratic colleagues. But this is what we have to do. And it is just the beginning. States around the nation must stand up to a federal government that constantly takes money from us only to bribe and coerce us into doing what it says.

Second, states must band together to fight against the intrusion of a federal government that seems to know no limit to its own wisdom. The health care law is the best example — and thankfully, numerous states around the country are fighting back through resolutions, legislation, and, probably more effectively, lawsuits. I am proud that Texas is part of that effort and will look for other ways to fight back. But there are other issues on which we must take a stand, such as the almost surreal effort by the federal government to stop Arizona from enforcing the law of the land with respect to immigration. Arizona is right to fight this in court and I expect it to continue to do so.

But probably most effective is for states to start telling Washington to enforce its own laws. When the federal government oversteps its authority, states should tell Washington that they will not be complicit in enforcing laws with which they do not agree. Again, the best example is an issue I don't even agree with — the partial legalization of marijuana. Californians clearly want some level of legalized marijuana, be it for medicinal use or otherwise. The federal government is telling them they cannot. But states are *not* bound to enforce federal law and the federal government cannot commandeer state resources and require them to enforce it.[6] So good luck to the federal government if it wants to enforce every law on its books without the help of state and local law enforcement. When the federal government oversteps its bounds, states should think hard about whether a single state resource should be committed to carry out the intrusive policy in question.

Finally, and most importantly, states must step up to the plate and both lead responsibly by example and develop innovative solutions to the complex issues we face as a people. And in many cases, states should band together to do so. Take for example, the issue of health care. As I stated before, we must repeal Obamacare, but we all agree that the health care system should be stronger. So we must be ready to answer the problems we face in our current systems. There is no reason that states cannot find ways to make insurance plans more affordable, with more options, with greater competition, and more portability across state lines. States can and should get together to find ways to make the health care system work regardless of what the federal government is doing.

States must also balance their budgets and show the kind of respect for local governance that they wish to see from Washington. In the end, states will not win every battle they choose to take on. There will be losses in court, and there will be money they can't necessarily turn down. But states can put pressure on the federal government to answer to the American people for its egregious unconstitutional overreach into their lives, and doing so is a critical part of the ability to take our country back.

3. Sustain a National Dialogue About Limited, Constitutional Government

My biggest motivator for writing this book is to help sustain a national dialogue about the proper structure and balance of government. When states take on the federal government, I am hopeful that it will jump-start a conversation about the importance of federalism in our system of government, and the need to restore the balance of power between the central and state governments.

This is paramount, because ultimately it is the people who get to decide how they choose to live and only by having this conversation will they be empowered to fight for the proper balance of power.

This conversation may start with governors and other state officials, but it should happen everywhere, from the schoolhouse down the road and all the way to Washington — and it should be carried out by teachers, talk radio hosts, college professors, politicians across every level, and around the dining room table at home. Few conversations on this earth are more important than one surrounding the question "Who gets to decide how we live?"

Our Founding Fathers risked everything they had to answer that question. The hundreds of thousands who died in the Civil War wrestled with that question. The hundreds of thousands who died in World Wars I and II, in Korea and in Vietnam, gave the last full measure of devotion to answer that question. And the current generation of patriots is declaring loudly to the world, as former President George W. Bush said they would, that it is not terrorists who decide how we live — it is the American people. The least we can do is to honor these great defenders of freedom with an ongoing dialogue, and to answer the question of who decides how we live here at home. Isn't that the country our patriots should come home to?

There are some good signs that the dialogue is beginning. Take, for example, the Tenth Amendment Task Force created in the House of Representatives and headed by Utah congressman Rob Bishop. This group seeks "to restore the constitutional balance of power through federalism."[7] The group, through Congressman Bishop, introduced a resolution honoring federalism in the summer of 2010 that began thusly: "Recognizing that the cause of liberty demands that government should be made accountable again to the consent of the governed, and calling for the real decentralization of power through the restoration of American federalism."[8]

What a good start.

4. Elect Leaders Who Respect the Constitution and Hold Them Accountable

In my first point about health care, I noted that we should support only politicians who will do what it takes to repeal Obamacare. But let's go further: anyone we elect must—and this is unequivocal—remain faithful to the Constitution and the limited government that it prescribes. Anything short of that is unacceptable.

"Fidelity to the Constitution" means exactly what it sound like it means. While there are some reasonable gray areas about which we can disagree, the text of the Constitution is hardly complicated and we are so far beyond the intent of the Founders with respect to so many aspects of our lives that there are few politicians in Washington who can reasonably claim to be faithfully upholding the Constitution. And truthfully, it's not hard to see who believes in the Constitution and who doesn't if we look closely.

For now, if you are an establishment politician in Washington, you'd better be prepared for a complete review of your record and every vote you take. That process is well under way already. We are seeing an energetic and important push by the American people—led in part by the Tea Party movement—to give the boot to the old-guard Washington establishment who no longer represent us. As I mentioned before, long-standing Utah senator Bob Bennett didn't even get renominated by Utah Republicans this year, in major part because he cosponsored a version of health care reform only slightly distinguishable from Obamacare. Arlen Specter fled the Republican Party because he knew he was going to be thrown out on his ear for his less-than-impressive record of fidelity to conservative principles, and he was later defeated in the Democratic Party primary.

Meanwhile, younger upstart conservatives are showing signs of establishing a new generation of Republicans eager to lead the nation on principle. Folks such as Nikki Haley in South Carolina, Bobby Jindal in Louisiana, Marco Rubio in Florida, Mike Lee in Utah, and a host of others are making waves throughout the nation. This is just the beginning. If candidates like these win, they should be held accountable too. But the lesson of their success in Republican primaries is that the American people are hungry for principled leadership. Following the 2010 elections, we must find candidates in 2012 who will support and defend the Constitution and hold all the newly elected representatives to account.

5. Adopt Certain Important Structural Reforms

If we have learned anything about the growth of Washington it is that politicians with power seek more of it. The difference between Republicans and Democrats is that Republicans will tell you they feel guilty about it. I believe we would do well to solidify the Founders' framework on federal power, and to help restore the proper balance between Washington and the states.

First, we must restrict federal spending. Rampant and wasteful spending in Washington is an affront to both freedom and federalism. The most important thing we could do is amend the Constitution—now—to restrict federal spending. There are generally thought to be two options: the traditional "balanced budget amendment" or a straightforward "spending limit amendment," either of which would be a significant improvement. I prefer the latter. It is imperative that we establish a constitutional requirement that the federal government live within its means like states and most American households must do—but I don't want the Washington establishment to hide behind tax increases to "balance" the budget. Let's use the people's document—the Constitution—to put an actual spending limit in place to control the beast in Washington.

But I also believe there are other important steps we should take. We should demand a complete overhaul of the appropriations process in Washington. I believe we need Congress to just stop doing anything at all for a while until it gets our fiscal house in order—in fact, possibly even calling a time-out, quickly passing the previous year's budget with an across-the-board cut in nondefense spending, and then using the time normally spent on appropriations to focus on balancing the budget, eliminating waste, and solving the entitlement crisis. In addition, I am in favor of a complete moratorium on earmarks until the budget is balanced, and perhaps permanently. And I believe our national budget process should be biennial, allowing oversight every other year, particularly during an election cycle. I think Washington could learn a thing or two from Texas, where our legislature meets once every two years for 140 days. While some joke it should be once every 140 years for two days, it's certainly miles better than what we have in Washington.

And we must demand an end to this federal strings game, in which dollars are sent from taxpayers to Washington only to be doled out according to the dictates of the federal government. One way to clean up the mess is to go back to block grants for transportation, education, and other areas in which the federal government has no business meddling. But even better, we should just stop the funneling of these funds through Washington in the first place. Let's send a clear message to Washington—stop telling us how to spend our money.

Second, we should restrict the unlimited source of revenue that the federal government has used to grow beyond its consti-

tutionally prescribed powers. One option would be to totally scrap the current tax code in favor of a flat tax, and thereby make taxation much simpler, easier to follow, and harder to manipulate. Another option would be to repeal the Sixteenth Amendment to the Constitution (providing the power for the income tax) altogether, and then pursue an alternative model of taxation such as a national sales tax or the Fair Tax. The time has come to stop talking about fixing the broken and burdensome tax code and to take bold action to replace it with one that is not a burden for the taxpayer and that provides only the modest revenue needed to perform the basic constitutional functions of the federal government. America needs a fairer, flatter, and simpler system, one which working families can complete without having to hire a bevy of professionals to assist them.

Third, we should take steps to restrict the unlimited power of the courts to rule over us with no accountability. There are a number of ideas about how to do this. Of course, the first thing we must do is support only nominees to the bench who actually believe in the Constitution. But we should also consider and ultimately adopt some actual reforms. One such reform would be to institute term limits on what are now lifetime appointments for federal judges, particularly those on the Supreme Court or the circuit courts, which have so much power. One proposal, for example, would have judges roll off every two years based on seniority. Other ideas include requiring the judges to have to stand for reappointment and reconfirmation. Another idea is to allow Congress to override the Supreme Court with a two-thirds vote in both the House and the Senate, which risks increased politicization of judicial decisions, but also has the benefit of letting the people stop the Court from unilaterally deciding policy.

Not as often discussed, but equally interesting, would be a "clarifying" amendment—or series of amendments—to the

Constitution. Such an amendment might, for example, clarify the scope and intent of the Fourteenth Amendment. As I have discussed, the Fourteenth Amendment is abused by the Court to carry out whatever policy choices it wants to make in the form of judicial activism. By passing a clarifying amendment, the people could speak with one voice about what powers they truly wish the federal government to have with respect to many important issues.

As limited as our federal government should be, we have unlimited opportunities to fix it. Whatever we do, we must proceed in a way that strengthens our constitutional system. By limiting the size and scope of Washington, we strengthen that system by restoring the proper power to states and the people. By taking these steps to ensure that the vision our Founders had for a limited central government is carried out, we can bring about a true renaissance of freedom in America, where the people once again control their lives without interference from faraway mandates in Washington. That is the very promise of America.

I believe that America is at a wonderful moment of awakening. The American people are seeing the consequences of decades of centralizing power in Washington, and they are ready to take their country back and restore the proper balance.

The people know that it isn't a powerful federal government that solves problems in their lives, but rather it is the people themselves. It is the people who create jobs, it is the people who cure diseases and invent new ways to solve complex problems, it is the people who take care of their families, it is the people who volunteer time and give money to charity, and it is the people who make the country work. And, knowing this, the American people see the benefit of self-government and government that is closer to the people. They see states that can balance their budgets, even in tough economic times, states that are solving real problems for the people every day, and states that are listening to the people and stepping up to fight an aggressive federal government that is failing, a sinking ship weighed down by the power it has amassed at the expense of our freedom.

The hope of America lies in its people. But the people can succeed only if they live freely in a country that honors its core principles of limited government, federalism, and a deep-seated commitment to liberty. Unfortunately, we are engaged in a fight to once again live in that country — and its future literally hangs in the balance. If not us, and if not now, then that hope is lost. The more layers the federal government piles on, the harder it is to go back.

Our fight is clear. We must retake the reins of our government from a Washington establishment that has abused our trust. We must empower states to fight for our beliefs, elect only leaders who are on our team, set out to remind our fellow Americans why liberty is guaranteed through a limited government set closest to the people, and take concrete steps toward these goals — starting first with the repeal of nationalized health care. The American people have never sat idle when liberty's trumpet sounds the call to battle — and today that battle is for the soul of America.

Our fight is to save America from Washington. The idea of America — enshrined in the greatest founding document of all time — is worth fighting for. We just need a few good patriots who are fed up with the status quo, armed with the Constitution, and fueled with courage to stand in the gap for future generations and to preserve for them the greatest beacon of hope, freedom, and prosperity the world has ever known.

AUTHOR'S NOTE

I want this book to help foster a nationwide conversation about the proper role of government in our lives. No organization that I am aware of is in a better to position to fight for this cause than the Texas Public Policy Foundation. In its 21 years, the Foundation has helped make Texas stronger while defending the Constitution and demonstrating the harm caused by the excesses of Washington. From Obamacare and rampant federal spending to the perils of environmental policy based on the hysteria of global warming, the Foundation has worked to chart a path for Texas to address these issues and others while reclaiming the rights reserved to the states and to our citizens.

Now, with its new Center for Tenth Amendment Studies and the leadership of former Texas solicitor general Ted Cruz and former Texas Supreme Court justice Scott Brister, the Foundation will provide even more support to Texans, citizens across the country, and elected officials in our fight to uphold and defend the Constitution. The Center was established to pursue restoration of respect for the Constitution's enumeration of powers so that government can be located closest to the people and so the right to life, liberty, and the pursuit of happiness may be preserved. This is exactly what we need today, because the spirit and intent of the Tenth Amendment—that all powers not specifically granted to the federal government are reserved to the states and to the people—is under assault and has been for some time. The result is that today we face unprecedented federal intrusion into numerous facets of our lives: from relationships with our doctors to the education of our children and our basic economic freedom.

Ronald Reagan said in his first inaugural address, "All of us need to be reminded that the federal government did not create the states; the states created the federal government." There is no better reminder of the importance of governing by this truth today than Texas, and the Foundation has played a tremendous role in helping Texas achieve its economic success of the last two decades. Therefore, to help bring the Tenth Amendment back to life in the twenty-first century, all of the author's net proceeds from the sale of this book will be donated to the Foundation to support the work of the Center for Tenth Amendment Studies. I am proud to partner with them to help ensure that Texas is a national leader in the cause of liberty and respect for a limited government.

ACKNOWLEDGMENTS

Where to begin my acknowledgments was a no-brainer because none of my political or philosophical pursuits would have been possible without my wife, Anita, encouraging me and standing by my side. I am blessed to have two wonderful adult children who keep me humble and have made their own sacrifices, with their father spending long days traveling Texas over the years. Griffin and Sydney, I will always treasure our days together and will be forever grateful for the enormity of your sacrifice so I could work to leave a better Texas for you and your generation.

I am appreciative of a number of people who have assisted me in the writing of this book. My friend and agent Jim Hornfischer encouraged me to write a definitive work on the Tenth Amendment at the time the Tea Party began to emerge and Americans began expressing a renewed enthusiasm for constitutional principles. I would be remiss not to point out that it was Craig Shirley who first advised me to write my first book, *On My Honor*. My political adviser of 13 years, David Carney, brought passion and vision to this project, and played an instrumental role in editing various chapters and assembling an extraordinary team. Invaluable research assistance was provided by Jerad Najvar and Amanda Hinson, two budding young lawyers, and we couldn't have written this book on such a compressed schedule if it weren't for their love of the law and the Constitution. I also want to express my gratitude to Rebecca Horner for assisting with our research efforts.

I owe a great deal to the folks at Little, Brown and Company for believing in the concept we brought to them, working so quickly to provide excellent insight and edits, and making this a top priority. I would like to specifically acknowledge executive editor John Parsley, who was a joy to work with, provided invaluable advice, and served as a masterly editor, helping us to reduce voluminous amounts of copy to the most critical arguments. I also want to thank publisher Michael Pietsch, editor in chief Geoff Shandler, and publicity director Heather Rizzo for helping us market *Fed Up!* to the public. I am thankful to my former communications director Eric Bearse for his friendship and his edits and ideas as well. Without the wise counsel of my friend Randy Erben I could not have put this book together, and I appreciate his efforts greatly. And I owe a debt of gratitude to Daniel Hodge, first deputy for Texas Attorney General Greg Abbott, for pointing out the numerous legal fronts, and cases, that demonstrate the encroachment of the federal government on state sovereignty.

I want to single out for special recognition Chip Roy, an outstanding legal scholar who previously served as senior adviser to U.S. Senator John Cornyn in his Senate leadership office and on the Senate Judiciary Committee, and who resigned his position as Special Assistant United States Attorney to devote himself full-time to the completion of the original manuscript. Writing a book of this nature in the midst of a campaign for reelection was a herculean task and wouldn't have been possible without Chip's dedication over the course of several months. He brought to this effort an amazing knowledge of the U.S. Constitution and other Founding documents, and a keen ability to frame federalist arguments in striking terms that make complicated law easier for non-lawyers like me to understand and discuss. Chip, it was a pleasure to work with you. You have a brilliant legal mind, and after working with you on this project I will never again attempt one like this without you by my side.

When my friend former House speaker Newt Gingrich offered to write the foreword to this book, I knew he would do a great job. But I did not know how well he would capture the fundamental point — that Washington is broken and our path to prosperity and freedom runs through the states and the people. Mr. Speaker, thank you. And I must also thank Peter Ferrara for his work in support of the Speaker in his effort.

Lastly, let me thank the millions of Texans, and the many more Americans, who are the true inspiration behind this book. You are the quiet majority that serves as the engine of progress. Many of you are so busy working one or more jobs, getting your children to soccer games and recitals, putting food on the table and giving back to your local community, that you may have assumed you could leave this country to the politicians. Many of you have now learned you can't — that Washington is heading down a dangerous course because it takes you for granted and opposes your values. The establishment thinks if they dole out enough pork and subsidies, you will ignore a century of constitutional erosion. But even a few inches a day amounts to miles of freedom of which you have been deprived as government grows larger. Your willingness to stand up, and say enough is enough, inspired this book. Your love for America, and the idea that we are a government that operates by the consent of the people, will get us through this dark chapter. It's your country, and your future, that Washington is meddling with. And I have a strong sense you are now fed up enough to do something about it. I wrote this book to voice your concerns, and partner with you in taking our country back.

NOTES

Chapter 1: America Is Great, Washington Is Broken

1. Charles Francis Adams, ed., *Familiar Letters of John Adams and His Wife Abigail Adams During the Revolution. With a Memoir of Mrs. Adams* (New York: Hurd and Houghton, 1876), 76.

2. Office of Management and Budget, Historical Tables, Table 1.1: "Summary of Receipts, Outlays, and Surplus or Deficits, 1789–2015," http://www.whitehouse.gov/omb/budget/historicals/. See also Christopher Chantrill, "United States Federal, State, and Local Spending," http://usgovernment spending.com.

3. James Gattuso and Stephen Keen, "Red Tape Rising: Federal Regulations in the Obama Years," Backgrounder 2394, Heritage Foundation, issued March 31, 2010, rev. April 8, 2010.

4. "Number of Words in the Internal Revenue Code and Federal Tax Regulations," Tax Foundation, Jan. 2006.

5. See http://www.thomas.gov. As of Aug. 30, 2010, in the 111th Congress 6,098 bills and resolutions had been introduced in the U.S. House and 3,753 bills in the U.S. Senate.

6. Jeffrey Passel and Paul Taylor, "Unauthorized Immigrants and Their U.S.–Based Children," Pew Hispanic Center, issued Aug. 11, 2010.

7. Citizens Against Government Waste, *2010 Congressional Pig Book,* http://www.cagw.org/assets/pig-book-files/2010/2010-pig-book-summary.pdf.

8. News Conference by President Obama, April 4, 2009, http://www.white house.gov/the-press-office/news-conference-president-obama-4042009.

9. "Be Heard: An MTV Discussion with Colin Powell," press conference held Feb. 14, 2002.

10. "Normandy American Cemetery and Memorial," pamphlet issued by the American Battle Monuments Commission, http://www.abmc.gov/cemeteries/cemeteries/nebase.pdf.
11. *CIA World Fact Book 2010,* https://www.cia.gov/library/publications/the-world-factbook/geos/us.html.
12. "United States Nobel Prize Winners," http://info.org/US_Nobel_Prizes.html.
13. "The 20 Largest Pharmaceutical Companies," Reuters, March 26, 2010, http://www.reuters.com/article/idUSN2612865020100326.
14. "Nobel Prizes in Physiology or Medicine," http://nobelprize.org/nobel_prizes/medicine/articles/lindsten-ringertz-rev/.
15. U.S. State Department, Annual Report of Immigrant and Visa Applicants Registered at the National Visa Center as of Nov. 1, 2009, http://travel.state.gov/pdf/WaitingListItem.pdf.
16. *The Index of Global Philanthropy and Remittances 2010,* Hudson Institute, http://www.hudson.org/files/pdf_upload/Index_of_Global_Philanthropy_and_Remittances_2010.pdf.
17. "Giving USA 2010: The Annual Report on Philanthropy for the Year 2009," Giving USA, Executive Summary, 4.

Chapter 2: Why States Matter

1. Thomas Jefferson, "Autobiography," in *Basic Writings of Thomas Jefferson,* ed. Philip S. Foner (New York: Willey Book Company, 1944), 464.
2. James Madison, Federalist No. 45: Bernard Bailyn, ed., *The Debates on the Constitution: Federalist and Antifederalist Speeches, Articles, and Letters During the Struggle Over Ratification* (New York: Library of America, 1993), vol. 2, 105.
3. Thomas Jefferson, Letter to Isaac H. Tiffany, in *Political Writings,* ed. Joyce Appleby and Terence Ball (New York: Cambridge University Press, 1999), 224.
4. Articles of Confederation, http://www.constitution.org/cons/usa-conf.htm.
5. James Madison, Federalist No. 39: Bailyn, *The Debates on the Constitution,* vol. 2, 30.
6. James Madison, Federalist No. 51: ibid., vol. 2, 160.
7. John P. Kaminski and Richard Leffler, eds., *Federalists and Antifederalists: The Debate Over the Ratification of the Constitution,* second edition (Madison, WI: Madison House, 1998), 164.
8. *U.S. v. Darby,* 312 U.S. 100 (1941).

9. Max Farrand, *The Framing of the Constitution of the United States* (New Haven, CT: Yale University Press, 1913), 91–112.

10. Paul Leicester Ford, ed., *Essays on the Constitution of the United States Published During the Discussion by the People, 1787–1788* (Brooklyn: Historical Printing Club, 1892), 64.

11. Michael R. Haines, "Population, Population Density, and Land Area, 1790–2000," Table Aa1-5, in Historical Statistics of the United States: Millennial Edition On Line.

12. Thomas Jefferson, Letter to Joseph C. Cabell, Feb. 2, 1816, in *The Writings of Thomas Jefferson,* vol. 13 (Thomas Jefferson Memorial Association, 1905), 205.

13. Office of the Clerk of the U.S. House of Representatives, "House History, 1st Congress," http://clerk.house.gov/art_history/house_history/index.html and U.S. Census Bureau, Historical Census Statistics on Population, Totals by Race, 1790 to 1990, for the United States Regions, Divisions, and States, Sept. 2002, http://www.census.gov/population/www/documentation/twps0056/twps0056.html, but note that this number represents all people, free and slave, voter and nonvoter.

14. U.S. Census Bureau, Historical Census Statistics on Population Totals by Race, 1790 to 1990, and by Hispanic Origin, 1970 to 1990, for the United States Regions, Divisions, and States, Sept. 2002, http://www.census.gov/population/www/documentation/twps0056/twps0056.html, noting again that the population number represents all people, free and slave, so the ratio for voters would have been even lower.

15. *New State Ice Co. v. Liebmann,* 285 U.S. 262 (1932).

16. Alexis de Tocqueville, *Democracy in America,* translated by Harvey C. Mansfield and Delba Winthrop (Chicago: University of Chicago Press, 2000), 57–58.

17. Matthew Spalding, *We Still Hold These Truths: Rediscovering Our Principles, Reclaiming Our Future* (Wilmington, DE: ISI Books, 2009), 136.

18. *Dred Scott v. Sandford,* 60 U.S. 393 (1857).

19. Mark Levin, *Liberty and Tyranny: A Conservative Manifesto* (New York: Threshold/Simon and Schuster, 2009), 59.

Chapter 3: What Happened to the Founders' Vision?

1. James Madison, *Writings,* ed. Jack N. Rakove (New York: Library of America, 1999), 355.

2. Talmadge Heflin, "Budget Driver: Federal Funds," Texas Public Policy Foundation Policy Perspective, Feb. 2010, 2.

3. Jonathan Weisman, "Wider U.S. Interventions Would Yield Winners, Losers as Industries Realign," *Wall Street Journal,* Nov. 20, 2008.

4. Woodrow Wilson, *The New Freedom: A Call for the Emancipation of the Generous Energies of a People* (New York: Doubleday, Page, 1913), 19–20.

5. "Carnegie's Estate, at Time of Death, about $30,000,000," *New York Times,* Aug. 29, 1919.

6. Kenneth W. Rose, "John D. Rockefeller," in *American National Biography,* vol. 18, ed. John A. Garraty and Mark C. Carnes (New York: Oxford University Press, 1999), 696.

7. John D. Buenker, "The Ratification of the Federal Income Tax Amendment," *Cato Journal,* spring 1981.

8. Gerald Prante, "Summary of Latest Federal Income Tax Data," *Fiscal Fact* 183, Tax Foundation, July 20, 2009.

9. "Top Marginal Tax Rates, 1913–2003," http://www.truthandpolitics.org.

10. "Treasury Department Gross Tax Collections: Amount Collected by Quarter and Fiscal Year, 1987–2007," Tax Policy Center (Urban Institute/ Brookings).

11. "State Houses Elect Senators," Historical Minute for June 7, 1917, http:// www.senate.gov/artandhistory/history/minute/State_Houses_Elect _Senators.htm.

12. Chester Collins Maxey, "A Little History of Pork," *National Municipal Review,* Dec. 1919.

13. *Hammer v. Dagenhart,* 247 U.S. 251 (1918).

14. Amity Schlaes, *The Forgotten Man: A New History of the Great Depression* (New York: HarperCollins, 2007), 151.

15. *A.L.A. Schechter Poultry Corp. v. U.S.,* 295 U.S. 495 (1935).

16. *NLRB v. Jones & Laughlin Steel Corp.,* 301 U.S. 1 (1937).

17. *Wickard v. Filburn,* 317 U.S. 111 (1942).

18. Alabama, "Song of the South," http://www.rhapsody.com/alabama/ greatest-hits-vol-2/song-of-the-south/lyrics.html.

19. Mona Charen, "That New New Deal," National Review Online, Nov. 28, 2008.

20. Burton W. Folsom Jr., *New Deal or Raw Deal: How FDR's Economic Legacy Has Damaged America* (New York: Threshold/Simon and Schuster, 2008), 249; Jim Powell, *FDR's Folly: How Roosevelt and His New Deal Prolonged the Great Depression* (New York: Crown Forum, 2003), viii.

21. Powell, *FDR's Folly,* viii.

22. Ibid.

23. Folsom, *New Deal or Raw Deal, 2.*
24. Ibid., 116.
25. Powell, *FDR's Folly,* 184.
26. Folsom, *New Deal or Raw Deal,* 117.
27. Powell, *FDR's Folly,* 184 (emphasis added).
28. Ibid., 186.
29. Milton Friedman, *Capitalism and Freedom* (Chicago: University of Chicago Press, 1962), 182–83.
30. *U.S. v. Lopez,* 514 U.S. 549 (1995); *U.S. v. Morrison,* 529 U.S. 598 (2000).
31. *Printz v. U.S.,* 521 U.S. 598 (1997).
32. *Gonzales v. Raich,* 545 U.S. 1 (2005).
33. Bailyn, *The Debates on the Constitution,* vol. 2, 167.
34. *U.S. v. Butler,* 297 U.S. 1 (1936).
35. *Steward Machine Co. v. Davis,* 301 U.S. 548 (1937).
36. *South Dakota v. Dole,* 483 U.S. 203 (1987).
37. Lynn Baker, "Conditional Federal Spending and States' Rights," *Annals of the American Academy of Political and Social Science,* March 2001.

Chapter 4: Washington Is Bankrupting America

1. "The Debt to the Penny and Who Holds It," http://www.treasurydirect.gov/NP/BPDLogin?application=np.
2. Projected national deficit for 2010 of $1.5 trillion divided by 365 days. See Bloomberg News, "Obama Raises 2010 Deficit Estimate to $1.5 Trillion," Aug. 25, 2010, http://www.bloomberg.com/apps/news?pid=newsarchive&sid=aNaqecavD9ek.
3. Brian Riedl, "Federal Spending by the Numbers," Special Report 79, Heritage Foundation, June 1, 2010.
4. Office of Management and Budget, Historical Tables, Table 7.1, "U.S. Federal Debt at the End of Year, 1940–2015."
5. Office of Management and Budget, Historical Tables, Table 3.1, "Outlays by Function and Superfunction, 1940–2015."
6. Laura Bassett, "Adm. Mike Mullen: 'National Debt Is Our Biggest Security Threat,'" http://www.huffingtonpost.com/2010/06/24/adm-mike-mullen-national_n_624096.html.
7. Lydia Saad, "Federal Debt, Terrorism Considered Top Threats to U.S.," http://www.gallup.com/poll/139385/federal-debt-terrorism-considered-top-threats.aspx.
8. Office of Management and Budget, Historical Tables, Table 3.1.

9. Office of Management and Budget, Historical Tables, Table 3.2, "Outlays by Function and Subfunction, 1962–2015."

10. Ibid.

11. Brian Riedl, "The Three Biggest Myths about Tax Cuts and the Budget Deficit," Backgrounder 2423, Heritage Foundation, June 21, 2010, 5.

12. Ibid., 10.

13. Kevin Williamson, "The Other National Debt," *National Review,* June 21, 2010, 28.

14. Allen Sloan, "Social Security, the Trust Fund, and Funny Money," *Washington Post,* Aug. 10, 2010.

15. David C. John, "Social Security's Deficits Reinforce the Need to Reform Spending," Webmemo 2727, Heritage Foundation, Dec. 10, 2009.

16. Ibid.

17. Williamson, "The Other National Debt," 28.

18. Mary Williams Walsh, "Social Security to See Payout Exceed Pay for This Year," *New York Times,* March 24, 2010.

19. Folsom, *New Deal or Raw Deal,* 118.

20. Ray Holbach and Alcestis "Cooky" Chang, "Galveston County: A Model for Social Security Reform," National Center for Policy Analysis, April 26, 2005.

21. Ibid.

22. Powell, *FDR's Folly,* 186.

23. Peter Keating, "Don't Believe the Hype on Medicare Part D," *Smart Money,* Sept. 2007.

24. Riedl, "Federal Spending by the Numbers," 8–9.

25. Jonathan Weisman and Jim VandeHei, "Road Bill Reflects the Power of Pork," *Washington Post,* Aug. 11, 2005.

26. Citizens Against Government Waste, *Congressional Pig Book 2010.*

27. Ibid.

28. Randal C. Archbold, "Ex-Congressman Gets 8-Year Term in Bribery Case," *New York Times,* March 4, 2006.

29. "Sen. Coburn Calls Earmarking Unconstitutional Abuse of Power," U.S. Federal News Service, March 13, 2008.

30. Riedl, "Federal Spending by the Numbers," 5; *Congressional Pig Book 2010.*

31. Suzanne Perry, "Senators Call on Boys and Girls Clubs of America to Justify Pay and Spending," *Chronicle of Philanthropy,* March 12, 2010; "Senators Work to Establish Accountability for Young People, Taxpayers," press release from the Senate Finance Committee, March 12, 2010.

32. Burton Folsom Jr., "The Origin of American Farm Subsidies," *The Freeman,* April 2006, 34.
33. Ken Cook, "Government's Continued Bailout of Corporate Agriculture," Environmental Working Group, http://farm.ewg.org/summary.php.
34. Riedl, "Federal Spending by the Numbers," 5.
35. Ibid.
36. Chris Edwards, "Milk Madness," Cato Institute, July 2003.
37. Ibid.
38. Dan Morgan, Sarah Cohen, and Gilbert M. Gaul, "Dairy Industry Crushed Innovator Who Bested Price Control System," *Washington Post,* Dec. 10, 2006, A1.
39. Ibid.
40. Ibid.
41. Ibid.
42. Ibid.
43. Thomas Lambie, "Miracle Down Under: How New Zealand Farmers Prosper Without Subsidies or Protection," *Cato Institute Free Trade Bulletin* 16, Feb. 7, 2005.
44. Steven Pakushin, "Japan May Relinquish Title of World's Highest Property Tax," Tax Foundation Tax Policy Blog, July 12, 2010.
45. Damian Paletta, "U.S. Lawmakers Reach Accord on New Finance Rules," *Wall Street Journal,* June 25, 2010.
46. Susan Page, "Most Americans OK with Big Government, at Least for Now," *USA Today,* April 15, 2009.
47. Jim Powell, "The 'Old' New Deal Still Isn't Paid For," *Forbes,* Feb. 11, 2009.
48. Riedl, "Federal Spending by the Numbers," 11.

Chapter 5: No American Left Alone

1. Ronald Reagan, "Televised National Address on Behalf of Senator Barry Goldwater, October 27, 1964" (also known as "A Time for Choosing"), in *Speaking My Mind: Selected Speeches* (New York: Simon and Schuster, 1989), 32.
2. N. C. Aizenman, "'Hard Work Begins' in Health Care Law's Details," *Washington Post,* June 3, 2010.
3. James Madison, Federalist No. 47: Bailyn, *The Debates on the Constitution,* vol. 2, 121.
4. Wilson, *The New Freedom,* 47.

5. Gary S. Lawson, "Limited Government, Unlimited Administration: Is It Possible to Restore Constitutionalism?," First Principles Series Report 23, Heritage Foundation, Jan. 27, 2009, 12.

6. Ibid., 12–13.

7. Bureau of Labor Statistics, "Career Guide to Industries, 2010–11 Edition: Federal Government."

8. Christopher Lee, "Big Government Gets Bigger," *Washington Post,* Oct. 6, 2006.

9. John Baker, "Revisiting the Explosive Growth of Federal Crimes," Legal Memorandum 26, Heritage Foundation, June 16, 2008.

10. Arthur B. Laffer and Stephen Moore, *Return to Prosperity: How America Can Regain Its Economic Superpower Status* (New York: Simon and Schuster, 2010), 92.

11. "Census Bureau Reports State and Local Government Employment Remains at 16.6 Million," U.S. Census Bureau press release, Aug. 31, 2010.

12. Bureau of Labor Statistics, "Career Guide to Industries, 2010–11 Edition: State and Local Government, Except Education and Health."

13. Ibid.

14. Nancy Benac, "Fact Check: Clinton, Obama, and Health Care," Associated Press, Jan. 23, 2008.

15. Fox News, "Anti-Abortion Groups Slam Administration Over Federal Funding for Pa. Health Plan," July 14, 2010, http://www.foxnews.com/politics/2010/07/14/anti-abortion-groups-slam-administration-federal-funding-pa-health-plan/.

16. Joint Economic Committee Minority Report, "America's New Health Care System Revealed," Aug. 2, 2010, http://jec.senate.gov/republicans/public/index.cfm?p=CommitteeNews&ContentRecord_id=bb302d88-3d0d-4424-8e33-3c5d2578c2b0.

17. "OMB Chief Orszag on Budgets and Their Discontents," speech to Economic Club of Washington, April 8, 2010.

18. Erick Erickson, "We Are No Longer a Nation of Laws: Senate Sets Up Requirement for Super-Majority to Ever Repeal Obamacare," http://www.redstate.com/erick/2009/12/21/we-are-no-longer-a-nation-of-laws-senate-sets-up-requirement-for-super-majority-to-ever-repeal-obamacare/.

19. David Leonhardt, "Saying No on Excessive Health Care," *New York Times,* April 8, 2010.

20. "European Leader Speaks Out About Government-Rule Health Care," *Hannity,* Fox News Channel, Aug. 12, 2009.

21. "Death Panels Begin to Take Shape," *Investors Business Daily* editorial, Aug. 19, 2010.

22. Ibid.

23. Ben Domenech, "Obama Nominee Donald Berwick's Radical Agenda," http://www.redstate.com/ben_domenech/2010/05/12/obama-nominee -donald-berwick%E2%80%99s-radical-agenda/.

24. Richard Foster, "Estimated Financial Effects of the Patient Protection and Affordable Care Act," Centers for Medicare and Medicaid Services, April 22, 2010.

25. *Cato Handbook for Policymakers,* seventh edition (Washington: Cato Institute, 2009), 126.

26. Letter from Congressional Budget Office director Douglas W. Elmendorf to Nancy Pelosi, March 20, 2010, http://cbo.gov/ftpdocs/113xx/doc11379/ AmendReconProp.pdf.

27. Terry Jones, "45% of Doctors Would Consider Quitting If Congress Passes Health Care Overhaul," *Investors Business Daily,* Sept. 15, 2009.

28. Michael D. Tanner, *Bad Medicine: A Guide to the Real Costs and Consequences of the New Health Care Law* (Washington: Cato Institute, 2010), 8–9.

29. Ibid.

30. Kevin Sack, "In Massachusetts, Universal Care Strains Coverage," *New York Times,* April 5, 2008.

31. Massachusetts Special Commission on the Health Care System, Minutes of Feb. 24, 2009, http.//www.mass.gov/Eeohhs2/docs/dhcfp/2009_02_24_ minutes.pdf.

32. Tanner, *Bad Medicine,* 31.

33. Letter from Douglas W. Elmendorf to Nancy Pelosi.

34. Ibid.

35. David Hilzenrath and N. C. Aizenman, "New Health-Care Rules Could Add Costs, Benefits to Some Insurance Plans," *Washington Post,* June 15, 2010.

36. Bryan Bollinger, Phillip Leslie, and Alan Sorensen, "Calorie Posting in Chain Restaurants," National Bureau of Economic Research Working Paper 15648, Jan. 2010.

37. National Automatic Merchandise Association Legislative Alert, Oct. 30, 2009, http://www.vending.org/pdf/NAMA_October_3,_2009_Leg_Alert.pdf.

38. General Accountability Office, "Education Finance: The Extent of Federal Funding in State Education Agencies," GAO/HEHS-95-3, Oct. 1994, 11, at http://archive.gao.gov/f0902a/152626.pdf.

39. Dan Lips and Evan Feinberg, "The Administrative Burden of No Child Left Behind," Webmemo 1406, Heritage Foundation, March 23, 2007.

40. Regina Umpstead, "No Child Left Behind Act: Is It an Unfunded Mandate or a Promotion of Federal Government Ideals?" *Journal of Law and Education,* April 2008, http://findarticles.com/p/articles/mi_qa3994/is_200804/ai_n25418939/pg_16/.

41. H.R. 1: No Child Left Behind Act of 2001, http://www.govtrack.us/congress/bill.xpd?bill=h107-1.

42. U.S. Department of Education, "Fiscal Year 2011 Budget Summary — February 1, 2010."

43. Elementary and Secondary Education Act, subpart 2, sec. 9527, Department of Education website, http://www2.ed.gov/policy/elsec/leg/esea02/pg112.html.

44. Alan Blinder, "House Seeks to Block Perry's School Action," *Houston Chronicle,* July 2, 2010.

45. James C. McKinley Jr., "A Clash in Texas Over Air Pollution," *New York Times,* June 9, 2010.

46. R. G. Ratcliffe, "EPA Rejects Air Permits of 122 Texas Plants," *Houston Chronicle,* July 1, 2010.

47. Letter from Gov. Perry to Pres. Obama, May 28, 2010.

48. Ibid.

49. Ibid.

50. State Rep. Byron Cook, "The EPA Needs to Stop Messing with Texas," *Austin American-Statesman,* June 21, 2010.

51. Kathleen Hartnett White, "Texas' Ozone Success: Changing Standards Mask Texas' Air Quality Achievements," Texas Public Policy Foundation, May 2010, http://www.texaspolicy.com/pdf/2010-05-RR04-Ozone-khw.pdf.

52. Greg Harman, "EPA vs. TCEQ: Texas Regulator's System Clouds Air-Quality Water," posted on "QueBlog," http://www.sacurrent.com, June 1, 2010.

53. Ibid. See also McKinley, "A Clash in Texas Over Air Pollution."

54. McKinley, "A Clash in Texas Over Air Pollution."

55. Stephen Power, "Senate Halts Effort to Cap Emissions," *Wall Street Journal,* July 23, 2010.

56. Ben Lieberman, "Small Business Impact of the Endangerment Finding," Webmemo 2766, Heritage Foundation, Jan. 20, 2010.

57. Ibid.

58. Ibid.

59. David Kreutzer and Karen Campbell, "CO$_2$-Emission Cuts: The Economic Costs of the EPA's ANPR Regulations," Heritage Foundation Center for Data Analysis Report 08-10, Oct. 29, 2008.
60. Elana Schor, "Efforts to Block the EPA's Greenhouse Gas Emissions Back in Play," *New York Times,* July 23, 2010.
61. "The Uncertainty Principle," editorial, *Wall Street Journal,* July 14, 2010.
62. "The Uncertainty Principle—II," editorial, *Wall Street Journal,* July 16, 2010.
63. Ibid.
64. "SEC Chairman Schapiro Announces Open Process for Regulatory Rule Making," Securities and Exchange Commission press release, July 27, 2010.

Chapter 6: Nine Unelected Judges Tell Us How to Live

1. Abraham Lincoln, First Inaugural Address, March 4, 1861, in *Speeches and Writings, 1859–1865,* ed. Don E. Fehrenbacher (New York: Library of America, 1989), 221.
2. Lino A. Graglia, "Constitutional Law Without the Constitution: The Supreme Court's Making of America," in *A Country I Do Not Recognize: The Legal Assault on American Values,* ed. Robert A. Bork (Stanford, CA: Hoover Institution Press, 2005), 3.
3. Charles Evans Hughes, "Speech Before the Elmira Chamber of Commerce, 1907," in *Addresses of Charles Evans Hughes, 1906–1916,* second edition (New York: Putnam, 1916), 183.
4. Letter to Nathaniel Macon, in *The Role of the Supreme Court in American Government and Politics, 1789–1935,* by Charles Grove Haines (Berkeley: University of California Press, 1944), 457–58.
5. Bork, Introduction, *A Country I Do Not Recognize,* x, xi.
6. *Kennedy v. Louisiana,* 554 U.S. 307 (2008).
7. See *Furman v. Georgia,* 408 U.S. 238 (1972), Constitution; U.S., amends. 5 and 8.
8. *Kennedy v. Louisiana* (2008), 36.
9. *Medellin v. Texas,* 552 U.S. 491 (2008).
10. *Van Orden v. Perry,* 545 U.S. 677 (2005).
11. *McCreary County, Kentucky v. American Civil Liberties Union of Kentucky,* 545 U.S. 844 (2005).
12. *Engel v. Vitale,* 370 U.S. 421 (1962); *School District of Abington Township, Pennsylvania v. Schempp,* 374 U.S. 203 (1963).
13. *Santa Fe Independent School District v. Doe,* 530 U.S. 290 (2000).

14. Ibid.
15. Liberty Legal Institute, "Examples of Hostility to Religious Expression in the Public Square," in Senate Judiciary Committee, Subcommittee on the Constitution, Civil Rights, and Property Rights, *Beyond the Pledge of Allegiance: Hostility to Religious Expression in the Public Square* (Washington: Government Printing Office, 2004), 156–73. The Liberty Legal Institute is now the Liberty Institute.
16. Ibid.
17. "Litigation," Boy Scouts of America National Council website, http://www.bsalegal.org/litigation-222.asp.
18. *U.S. v. Lopez* (1995).
19. Ibid.
20. *District of Columbia v. Heller,* 554 U.S. 570 (2008).
21. *McDonald v. Chicago,* 130 S. Ct. 3020 (2010).
22. *Griswold v. Connecticut,* 381 U.S. 479 (1965).
23. *Roe v. Wade,* 410 U.S. 113 (1973).
24. Steven Erhelt. "Analysis Shows 52 Million Abortions Since Supreme Court's *Roe v. Wade* Decision," Lifenews.com, Jan. 22, 2010, http://www.lifenews.com/nat5910.html.
25. *Lawrence v. Texas,* 539 U.S. 558 (2003).
26. *Planned Parenthood v. Casey,* 505 U.S. 833, 851 (1992).
27. Bork, Introduction, *A Country I Do Not Recognize,* xviii.
28. *Lawrence v. Texas* (2003).
29. *Goodridge v. Mass. Department of Public Health,* 440 Mass. 309 (2003).
30. *League of United Latin American Citizens v. Perry,* 548 U.S. 399, 511 (2006).
31. Ibid.
32. Abigail Thernstrom, "Divvying Up," *Wall Street Journal,* June 29, 2006.
33. *U.S. v. Virginia,* 518 U.S. 515 (1996).
34. *McConnell v. FEC,* 540 U.S. 93 (2003); *Cohen v. California,* 518 U.S. 515 (1971).
35. Graglia, "Constitutional Law Without the Constitution," 22.

Chapter 7: The Federal Government Fiddles

1. Joseph Story, *Commentaries on the Constitution of the United States. With a Preliminary Review of the Constitutional History of the Colonies and States, Before the Adoption of the Constitution* (Boston: Williams, Grey, 1833), vol. 1, 383.

2. Maggie Ybarra and Adriana Gomez Licon, "Mexican Authorities: Federal Agents Could Have Fired Bullets into City Hall," *El Paso Times,* July 2, 2010.

3. Diana Washington Valdez, "Bullet Strikes UTEP; Natalicio: Campus Not Target," *El Paso Times,* Aug. 23, 2010.

4. Ioan Grillo, "Special Report: 7 Circles of Juarez," http://www.globalpost.com, posted July 13, 2010. The correct figure is 5,500 murders between Jan. 2008 and July 2010.

5. Jason Beauben, "Grief, Rage Fuel Mothers' Search for Justice," NPR, March 15, 2010.

6. U.S. State Department, Bureau for International Narcotics and Law Enforcement Affairs, *International Narcotics Control Strategy Report, Volume 1: Drug and Chemical Control,* 432.

7. Susana Hayward, "A Report from Juarez, Mexico, the Bleeding Front Line in the War on Drugs," *Phoenix New Times,* May 6, 2010.

8. Andrew Chung: "Ciudad Juarez, Mexico: The World's Most Dangerous Place?," *Toronto Star,* May 21, 2010.

9. Richard Martel, "U.S. Charges Top Leaders of Tijuana-Based Drug Cartel," *Los Angeles Times,* July 24, 2010.

10. "Mexico Under Siege: Interactive Map," *Los Angeles Times,* http://projects.latimes.com/mexico-drug-war/#/its-a-war.

11. "Pinal Co. Deputy Shot by Illegal Immigrants in Desert," http://www.myfoxphoenix.com, April 30, 2010.

12. Ybara and Licon, "Mexican Authorities."

13. John D. Skrentny, "Immigration Reform: Start with Small Steps," CNN.com (July 13, 2010).

14. Department of Homeland Security, Office of Immigration Statistics, "Estimates of the Unauthorized Immigrant Population Residing in the United States: Jan. 2009," 1 (published Jan. 2010).

15. Ibid., 4.

16. Jeffrey Passel and D'Vera Cohn, "Mexican Immigrants: How Many Come? How Many Leave?" Pew Hispanic Center, July 22, 2010.

17. "The Impact of Unauthorized Immigrants on the Budgets of State and Local Governments," Congressional Budget Office 1 (Dec. 2007).

18. "Special Report: Undocumented Immigrants in Texas: A Financial Analysis of the Impact to the State Budget and Economy," Office of the Comptroller (Dec. 2006).

19. Ibid., 20.

20. Ibid.

21. Ibid., 69.

22. Ibid., 137.

23. Howard Fischer, "Napolitano, Brewer Huddle at Governor's Meeting," *East Valley Tribune,* July 11, 2010.

24. Janet Napolitano, "'Stimulus' and the States," *Wall Street Journal,* April 24, 2008.

25. Congressional Budget Office, *The Impact of Unauthorized Immigrants,* 3.

26. Perry Bacon Jr. and Anne E. Kornblut, "Issue of Illegal Immigration Is Quandary for Democrats: Many Voters Want Tougher Stance Than Candidates Offer," *Washington Post,* Nov. 2, 2007.

27. Matt Mayer and Jane Baker McNeill, "Time to Stop the Rush for 'Amnesty' Immigration Reform," Backgrounder 2385, Heritage Foundation, July 29, 2010.

28. Ibid., 4–6; Center for Immigration Studies commentary.

29. "Cop Killing Sparks Immigration Debate," ABC News, Sept. 25, 2006. See also Susan Cornell, "Quintero Case a Battle Cry Against Illegal Immigration," *Houston Chronicle,* May 21, 2008.

30. James Pinkerton and Susan Carroll, "Officer's Killer No Stranger to Police," *Houston Chronicle,* June 26, 2009. The illegal alien had been deported ten years earlier and had been ticketed by the cops four times before he killed the cop.

31. Mayer and McNeill, "Time to Stop the Rush for 'Amnesty' Immigration Reform."

32. Hans van Spakovsky, "A Broken Immigration Court System," "The Foundry" blog, Heritage Foundation, posted June 21, 2010.

33. Michael D. Shear and Spencer S. Hsu, "President Obama to Send More Troops to U.S.–Mexico Border," *Washington Post,* May 26, 2010.

34. *U.S.–Mexico Border Counties Coalition, Undocumented Immigrants in U.S.–Mexico Border Counties,* 3.

35. Dave Montgomery, "Border Deployment 'On Track,' Guard Says," *Fort Worth Star-Telegram,* Aug. 11, 2010.

36. Sandra Erwin, "Five Key Questions About the Defense Budget," *National Defense,* Aug. 2010.

37. "Eisenhower Library (Defense Spending)," speech delivered by Secretary of Defense Robert M. Gates, May 8, 2010.

38. Ibid.

39. Erwin, "Five Key Questions About the Defense Budget."

40. Noah Shachtman, "The Air Force Needs a Serious Upgrade," *Wall Street Journal,* July 15, 2010, A17.

41. Ibid.

42. Ibid.

43. Ibid. Also, Andrew Krepinevich of the Center for Strategic and Budgetary Assessments says our procurement strategy has resulted in a "hollow buildup" that doesn't achieve modernization. See quotes in Erwin, "Five Key Questions About the Defense Budget."

44. Brett Schaefer, "National Security Goes Green," Commentary, Heritage Foundation, Feb. 11, 2010.

45. Speech by Pres. Obama, Prague, Czech Republic, April 5, 2009, http://www.whitehouse.gov/the_press_office/Remarks-By-President-Barack-Obama-In-Prague-As-Delivered/.

46. David Kay, "Weapons Inspectors Can't Disarm Iran," *Wall Street Journal* op-ed, July 17, 2010, A11.

47. *This Week,* ABC, June 27, 2010.

48. R. James Woolsey and Rebeccah Heinrichs, "Iran and the Missile Defense Imperative," *Wall Street Journal,* July 14, 2010.

49. *This Week.*

50. Woolsey and Heinrichs, "Iran and the Missile Defense Imperative."

51. Ibid.

52. Marc Chapman and Peter Spiegel, "U.S. Missile U-Turn Roils Allies," *Wall Street Journal,* Sept. 18, 2009.

53. Ibid.

54. "New Start: Romney Was Right," *National Review* editorial, July 12, 2010.

55. "NASA Chief: Next Frontier Better Relations with Muslim World," Fox News.com, July 5, 2010.

56. Andy Pasztor, "NASA Program Remains Uncertain After Budget Vote," *Wall Street Journal,* June 30, 2010.

57. Dana Priest and William Arkin, "Top Secret America: A Hidden World Growing Beyond Control," *Washington Post,* July 19, 2010.

58. Ibid.

59. "National Intelligence Director Dennis Blair Stepping Down," Associated Press, May 20, 2010.

60. Priest and Arkin, "Top Secret America."

61. James Gordon Meek, "Attorney General Eric Holder: Politics Plagues Khalid Sheikh Mohammed Trial, Guantanamo Closing," *New York Daily News,* July 11, 2010.

62. L. Gordon Crovitz, "Government Drops the Ball on Patents," *Wall Street Journal* op-ed, July 19, 2010.

Chapter 8: Standing Athwart History

1. Patrick Henry, Speech to the Virginia Convention, in *Sketches of the Life and Character of Patrick Henry,* by William Wirt (Philadelphia: James Webster, 1817), 120, http://docsouth.unc.edu/southlit/wirt/wirt.html.
2. *National Review,* September 30, 1955.
3. Max Farrand, ed., *The Records of the Federal Convention of 1787,* revised edition (New Haven, CT: Yale University Press, 1937), vol. 1, 584.
4. Mayhill Fowler, "Obama: No Surprise That Hard-Pressed Pennsylvanians Turn Bitter," Huffington Post, April 11, 2008, http://www.huffingtonpost.com/mayhill-fowler/obama-no-surprise-that.ha_b_96108.html.
5. Ezra Klein, "Nancy Pelosi's Strategy for Passing Health Care Reform," blog entry posted at http://www.washingtonpost.com, March 15, 2010.
6. http://twitter.com/JimDeMint/status/19104956597.
7. Edwin Feulner, "Taxpayers Cooked," *Washington Times,* June 16, 2008.
8. Clip broadcast on *The O'Reilly Factor,* April 2, 2010.
9. David Cho, Jia Lynn Yang, and Brady Dennis, "Lawmakers Gird Dodd-Frank Bill for Wall Street Reform into Homestretch," *Washington Post,* June 26, 2010.
10. Robert Pear, "Senate Passes Health-Care Overhaul on Party-Line Vote," *New York Times,* Dec. 24, 2009.
11. Jared Allen and Jeffrey Young, "House Sends Senate Healthcare Bill to Obama's Desk after 219–212 Vote," *The Hill,* March 21, 2010.
12. W. James Antle III, "The Disappearing Pro-Life Democrat," posted on http://www.spectator.org, March 22, 2010.
13. Steven Erfelt, "Obama Administration OK's First Tax-Funded Abortions under Health Care Law," posted on http://www.lifenews.com, July 13, 2010.
14. Douglas E. Kneeland, "Ability Is Issue in New Hampshire Race," *New York Times,* Feb. 7, 1976.
15. Jeffrey Gayner, "The Contract with America: Implementing New Ideas in the U.S.," Heritage Foundation lecture, Oct. 13, 1995.
16. Office of Management and Budget, Historical Tables, Table 3.1, "Outlays by Function and Superfunction."
17. Fred Barnes, "A 'Big Government Conservatism,'" *Wall Street Journal,* Aug. 15, 2003.
18. George Will, "Socialism, It's Already Here," *Washington Post,* Nov. 16, 2008, B7.

19. Shikha Dalmia, "No Child Left Behind Act: Keep It or Kill It?" Reason Foundation, Dec. 13, 2007.
20. Office of Management and Budget, "Outlays by Function and Superfunction."
21. Citizens Against Government Waste, "Pork Trends, 1991–2009."
22. Pamela Villarreal, "Social Security and Medicare Projections: 2009," National.Center for Policy Analysis, June 11, 2009.
23. http://www.govtrack.us/congress/bill.xpd?bill=h108-1.
24. http://www.govtrack.us/congress/bill.xpd?bill=h110-1424.
25. Robert Draper, "Lindsay Graham, This Year's Maverick," *New York Times Magazine,* July 1, 2010.
26. Jordan Fabian, "Bennett: My Defeat Was Not 'Logical,'" blog entry posted at http://thehill.com, May 13, 2010. I think it's stronger to quote Sen. Bennett's claim that he lost because "I was in Washington" and Tea Party voters "hate Washington."
27. Shelagh Murray, "Republican Lawmakers Gird for Rowdy Tea Party," *Washington Post,* July 18, 2010.
28. Jeffrey M. Jones, "Low Approval in Congress Points to High Seat Change in November," Gallup, June 24, 2010.
29. "Congressional Performance," Rasmussen Reports, Aug. 9, 2010.
30. "72% of GOP Voters Say Republicans in Congress Out of Touch with Their Base," Rasmussen Reports, June 16, 2010.
31. "Congressional Performance," Rasmussen Reports.
32. Lydia Saad, "Congress Rates Last in Confidence in Institutions," Gallup, July 22, 2010.

Chapter 9: States Do the Work of the People

1. Thomas Jefferson, Letter to Charles Hammond, August 18, 1821, in *The Writings of Thomas Jefferson,* ed. Andrew A. Lipscomb (Washington: Thomas Jefferson Memorial Association, 1903), vol. 15, 332.
2. Senate Committee on Homeland Security and Governmental Affairs, *Hurricane Katrina: A Nation Still Unprepared* (Washington: Government Printing Office, 2006), 70.
3. Ibid.
4. "Harris County, Texas, Citizen Corps' Response to Hurricane Katrina," http://www.fema.gov/pdf/emergency/nims/lessons_learned_tx_katrina.pdf.
5. Jeff Opdyke, Gary McWilliams, and Michael Schneider, "The Next Deluge," *Wall Street Journal,* Sept. 1, 2005.

6. "Harris County, Texas, Citizen Corps' Response to Hurricane Katrina."
7. Ibid.
8. Ibid.
9. Don Bustillus, "Public Health Emergency Powers in the Aftermath of Hurricane Katrina," http://www.law.uh.edu/healthlaw/perspectives/September2005/(DB)KatrinaandPublicHealth.pdf.
10. Trymaine Lee, "Making the Grade," *New Orleans Times-Picayune,* March 3, 2000.
11. Susan Page, "Evacuees Shun Going Home," *USA Today,* Oct. 13, 2005.
12. "Texas Agrees to Accept 50,000 More from La.," Associated Press, Sept. 1, 2005, http://www.msnbc.msn.com/id/9152644/ns/us_news-katrina_the_long_road_back/.
13. Lisa Falkenberg, "Perry Staffers' Email Recorded Katrina Turmoil," *Houston Chronicle,* Jan. 22, 2006.
14. "Testimony of Jeb Bush, Governor of the State of Florida, Before the House Committee on Homeland Security," Oct. 19, 2005, http://www.floridadisaster.org/documents/testimony_10-19-2005.pdf.
15. "Governor Jindal Calls on the Feds to Get in the War to Win It," States News Service, June 28, 2010.
16. Gary Perilloux, "Triton Tackles Oil Leak," *Baton Rouge Advocate,* July 18, 2010.
17. "Governor Jindal Calls on the Feds."
18. Texas Commission on Environmental Quality, http://tceq.state.tx.us/about/tceqhistory.html.
19. Vernon Trollinger, "How Texas Energy Deregulation Leads the Way for Innovation (Part I)," http://ezinearticles.com.
20. Tom Fowler, "Texas Still Leads U.S. in Wind Power — But There's New Competition," posted at "News Watch Energy" blog, http://www.chron.com, April 8, 2010.
21. Jordan Fabian, "Top Republican: Fiscal Commission Putting Tax Hikes 'On the Table,'" blog entry posted at http://thehill.com, July 22, 2010.
22. Elizabeth McNichol, Phil Oliff, and Nicholas Johnson, "Recession Continues to Batter State Budgets; State Responses Could Slow Recovery," Center for Budget and Policy Priorities, July 11, 2010.
23. Interview with Gov. Bob McDonnell, broadcast on *Hannity,* Fox News Channel, July 14, 2010.
24. "Chris Christie's Compromise," *Economist,* July 15, 2010.

25. Ibid.
26. Stephen Dinan, "Holder Hasn't Read Bill He Criticized," *Washington Times,* May 13, 2010.
27. William McQuillan, "Arizona Will Appeal Ruling on Immigration Law, Judge Says," Bloomberg, July 29, 2010.
28. "Gov. Perry Backs Resolution Affirming Texas' Sovereignty Under 10th Amendment," press release issued April 9, 2009, http://governor.state.tx .us/news/press-release/12227/.
29. http://www.thenewamerican.com/index.php/usnews/health-care/3176 -states-legislators-and-citizens-resist-obamacare.
30. "The States' Lawsuit Challenging the Constitutionality of the Health Care Reform Law," http://www.healthcarelawsuit.us/webfiles.nsf/WF/MRAY -83TKWB/$file/HealthCareReformLawsuit.pdf.
31. "Right to Carry 2010," National Rifle Association Institute for Legislative Action, http://www.nraila.org/Issues/factsheets/read.aspx?ID=18.
32. Ion Urbina, "Fearing Federal Agenda, States Rush to Loosen Gun Laws," *New York Times,* Feb. 24, 2010.
33. *Gonzales v. Raich* (2005).
34. Ibid.
35. *Printz v. U.S.* (1997).
36. "Pot Legalization Gains Momentum in California," Associated Press, Oct. 7, 2009, http://cbs5.com/politics/california.marijuana.legalize.2.1234298.html.
37. Letter to the Texas Congressional Delegation, July 29, 2010, Gov. Rick Perry et al.
38. Gov. Rick Perry, "Rejecting Race to the Top Funds Was an Easy Call," *Austin American-Statesman,* Feb. 4, 2010.

Chapter 10: Retaking the Reins of Government

1. Abraham Lincoln, "Address to the Young Man's Lyceum Association," January 27, 1838, in *Speeches and Writings,* 32.
2. Jefferson, Letter to Charles Hammond.
3. James Madison, Federalist No. 62: Bailyn, *The Debate on the Constitution,* vol. 2, 249.
4. Jonathan Elliot, ed., *The Debates in the Several State Conventions on the Adoption of the Federal Constitution as Recommended at the General Convention at Philadelphia in 1787,* second edition (Philadelphia: Lippincott, 1866), vol. 4, 431.

5. "The President's News Conference, January 29, 1981," in *Public Papers of the Presidents of the United States: Ronald Reagan* (Washington: Government Printing Office, 1982), 56.

6. *Printz v. U.S.* (1997).

7. "House Republicans Launch New 10th Amendment Task Force," press release from Rep. Rob Bishop, May 1, 2010, http://robbishop.house.gov/News/DocumentSingle.aspx?DocumentID=184458.

8. House Resolution 1587, introduced by Rep. Bishop, July 30, 2010.

INDEX

INDEX

INDEX

INDEX

ABOUT THE AUTHOR

RICK PERRY has served as governor for ten years — longer than any other in Texas history — and before being elected he served in the Texas legislature, as the Texas Agricultural Commissioner, and as lieutenant governor. Perry has been in the leadership of the Republican Governors Association for five years and is an Eagle Scout. After he graduated from Texas A&M, he became an Air Force pilot and attained the rank of captain.